Halfway Through the Door

BOOKS BY ALAN ARKIN

Halfway Through the Door

*An Actor's Journey
Toward the Self*

Alan Arkin

HARPER & ROW, PUBLISHERS

New York, Hagerstown, San Francisco, London

FIRST EDITION

Designer: Stephanie Winkler

Library of Congress Cataloging in Publication Data

Arkin, Alan.
  Halfway through the door.
  1. Yoga. I. Title.
B132.Y6A68   181'.45   78–20154
ISBN 0–06–010133–4

79 80 81 82 83 10 9 8 7 6 5 4 3 2 1

When I asked my guru if this book could be dedicated to him, the answer was yes, with the understanding that he in turn would dedicate the book to his guru, he to his, and on and on, like ripples in a pond and ending at a shore that I cannot begin to imagine.

This book is dedicated to my guru.

Halfway Through the Door

Introduction

The main body of my work in yoga takes place in meditation and under the careful guidance of my guru, but I have found much help from reading in and around the work we are doing. Hermann Hesse, Dr. John Lilly, Richard Alpert, Carlos Castaneda, Paramahansa Yogananda and many others have whetted my curiosity about the nature of reality and my possibilities for growth, and their books have spurred me on to deeper work with my teacher. He has not been terribly enthusiastic about my reading, feeling that most of it is intellectualizing a process that should really be experienced viscerally, but he understands my nature and my needs, and so my library grows. But in all the volumes that I have pored over, I have never come across anything that deals with the early stages: the changes that occur in the first few years of work, before anything like enlightenment takes place.

It would be exciting to read a chronicle by a highly developed soul that began with his first few meditations and recorded each significant development as it happened. It would be exciting for many reasons. Among other things, we would sense the tremendous increases in energy that would fill the author periodically, take hold, and then be succeeded by an even greater burst of power. We would see neurotic patterns disappear slowly, emotional disturbances die down. We would see shifts in literary style and rhythm. New vocabulary would appear. The person's relationship to his personality would change: he would stop being buffeted and battered by his own nature and the forces around him, begin climbing out of his confusion, and eventually we would feel him basking in light so profound that all descriptions would disappear, and we would be left only with expressions of joy, accompanied by a complete lack of desire to write anything at all; for the more liberated a person becomes, the more inadequate is language. Advanced souls have to speak of union with the infinite in language more suitable for automobile repair manuals, and all we have to go on ultimately is a hint of their energy, or descriptions written about them by friends or disciples.

Carlos Castaneda does a brilliant job of describing his early advance, as does Dr. John Lilly, but they both took drugs in the beginning stages of their work, and in general used methods that would be terrifying to the average person embarking on a path of enlightenment; there are fears enough in a gentle and orthodox approach toward yoga. I do not pretend to be a liberated soul or anything like it, which in terms of this little book is probably a good thing, as I still have the frame of reference and the vocabulary of someone adrift in the great existential sea, where most sensitive, intelligent people wind up before finding an anchor in a greater reality. As you will see, I had enormous misgivings about embarking on a spiritual path. My resistance is mostly gone now, but the memory of my pain and confusion is still vivid enough so that the reader may find some comfort in seeing what I came out of and what can be overcome. Liberation is an inch-by-inch proposition. Perhaps a dozen times in the history of man it has happened in an instant. Spontaneously. This has certainly not been the case with me. But the advances I have made in a few years have felt so profound that the me I write about at the beginning of the book begins to feel like a stranger. It is important to point out that I am not special. What has been given to me is available to all mankind and for all time. All that is necessary is to want it. What I write here is all true. It is addressed to those people who will sense its veracity with a part of themselves that now only whispers to them. It is written in the hope that these words may be of some small help in turning that whisper into a roar.

We have all had transcendental experiences. They can be had while painting a picture, playing tennis, making love, cooking a meal, writing a letter, building a birdhouse or singing a song. They are those rare moments when we are operating past our abilities. They are the most exhilarating moments in life. It is as if we are not responsible for our own actions but are witnessing them from some exalted vantage point. In these states we seem to be able to do no wrong. Unfortunately, they don't last very long, and we have no apparent control over their comings and goings.

For me the craft of acting was for many years a source of transcendental experiences. On stage I was able to have these moments with a certain amount of frequency, and so my life revolved more and more around acting in films and in the theater. This became virtually my one source of joy. The experience of being onstage and having my character take over, to have him lead me around as if I were riding the crest of an enormous wave, disassociated from time, from the need for approval, from the fear of failing, from the fear of crowds, from anxiety over the future or the possibility of any aggressive act I might take—this was ecstasy. What I ended up doing, as do most people who are fortunate enough to have a talent like this, was to live my life in constant dedication to my craft.

The theater became my addiction, my obsession, my god. What I did not realize—and this is crucial—is that there is no power whatsoever in the craft of acting itself. Acting is nothing more than a concept. The power I experienced on stage was in me. I invested my performances with that power. Had I been courageous enough to accept the idea that the power was mine to invest anywhere I chose, in whatever craft, sport, profession, social activity, I would have been a much happier person much sooner. But I kept this knowledge from myself. And the reason I did so was because power is dangerous, and I did not trust myself to use it well. Therefore the stage, where all manner of hateful or beautiful things can take place and no one gets hurt.

Interestingly, I began to lose that power when my name was placed over the title of a play. When I became a star, all of a sudden I could no longer lose myself in a character. I could no longer hide, because people were coming to the theater to see *me*. I was forced to accept the fact that I was not really the character I was portraying, that I was actually on stage, and that the feelings I displayed were really variations of my own emotions. This stifled me to the point that it became uncomfortable to be in front of an audience. I began holding myself carefully in check. I became afraid of taking chances, of having the audience dislike me. And as a result, my flights of liberation now came only with sex, alcohol or marijuana. Fortunately, I was able to work in film, which is more intimate, and although there is never enough time from shot to shot to have an extended feeling of flight, there is still a wonderful fantasy life built around the idea of being a successful actor. Most of these fantasies involved the anticipation of more money, more attention, more ability to control associates, scripts; and for a while all this sustained me. I was not happy, mind you, but I was terribly busy.

At this time, I was in analysis with a doctor who was kind,

wise and deeply responsible, and although I do not remember talking specifically about it, the underlying idea of the whole analytic experience seemed to be leading toward being able to function in a career, and to love one or two people. Happiness didn't seem to enter into it. Initially I was concerned simply with not being miserable, but as time went on, this view of life started feeling very meager. I felt a need for more to strive toward. I wanted life to hold more promise. Another source of discomfort was my doctor's claim that he had faced the idea of his own death, his complete extinction, total annihilation. I was not able to do this, nor could I really believe that he had done so. I did not have a religious bent; I was simply not able to face the idea of the snuffing out of all consciousness. My inability to do so I chalked up to infantilism and fear.

I possessed an enormous amount of hidden rage, which six years of analysis had not stirred. I made every attempt to outsmart my anger, to joke it out of existence, to anticipate it, to rationalize my way around it. But it was an energy that would not be denied, and it expressed itself in other ways, such as constant headaches, stomach trouble, sinus problems, and on and on. Try as I might—and my doctor said on several occasions that I was working very hard—I could not trap myself into a full exposé of what was going on inside me.

I have a high regard for analysis and what it did for me. It curbed what felt like suicidal tendencies, got me out of a pattern of very destructive relationships with women, relieved a great deal of paranoia and allowed me to really listen to people for the first time in my life. These are great and wonderful things, and I thank my doctor from the bottom of my heart for helping me over these hurdles, but the thing I thank him most deeply for I don't think he would understand or appreciate, and that is for helping me find the courage to face my teacher, my guru.

Curiously, I met my teacher right around the time that I started analysis. I was doing a guest appearance on a television show called *East Side, West Side,* which starred George C. Scott. John was a bit player—I don't think he had any lines—and I gravitated toward him because he was someone to whom I could complain, and who would listen. He seemed bright and sensitive, and at the time I felt he was somewhat morose, but I realize now that I attributed this quality to him because it was one of my own outstanding features. I had a gloomy and pessimistic nature and enjoyed sharing it. Since I was drawn to John, I had to imbue him with this quality to ensure that we had something in common: things to complain about. My feelings in no way reflected what he was experiencing. I remember little else of him during that week except that he helped me at one point through some terrible tension by giving me a long breathing exercise, and then a few days later, apropos of a mutual interest in photography, he invited me to his home in Mount Vernon to use his darkroom.

It was symptomatic of my condition that his kindness and generosity was suspect to me. My mind turned in two directions. Either he was trying to use me as a stepping stone in his career, or he was a homosexual. The idea of his simply liking me, caring about me, wanting to spend time with me because I was in some way valued, did not enter my mind. It took six years of intensive work in analysis before I could even consider these possibilities and was ready to meet him again. Even then I did not recognize him as my teacher.

In 1968 I was playing the title role in a film called *Popi.* It was a film I cared about deeply. I felt I was doing good work, I was making a great deal of money, and I was in a period of my career when I was popular and in demand. My marriage was thriving. I had, in fact, achieved everything I had ever set out to do. Through my own efforts and with the help of analysis, I had realized a life that would have been the envy of most of the world. The one problem I could not work around was that I was angry and unhappy most of the time. I was all right as long as I was acting, making love, eating and buying some piece of musical or photographic equipment, but the rest of the time I was actively confused and empty.

Had I been able to busy myself twenty-four hours a day with creative projects, lovemaking and eating, I probably could have avoided yoga. But sooner or later in the day there was that moment when I was alone or exhausted, and then the endless nightmare of "Who am I?" would present itself. I knew people who seemed to be able to avoid this nightmare, people who had decided on their limits, the areas in which they were comfortable and those in which they were not. People who simply refused to allow their minds any excursions into unknown territory. I had friends who maintained that they had a clear idea of who they were in the universe, and seemed to be able to live reasonably well in and around their beliefs.

I found myself envying these people with fixed goals, fixed identities. I would have traded places with any number of them, but I could not. They had an ability that I did not possess. A moment alone, a bad review, a play closing—any one of a hundred things could send me into oblivion. And yet somewhere, even in my darkest moments, I suspected that I knew something they did not know, that lurking in my despair and questioning was more truth than in their rigid certainties.

Sometime during the first few weeks of filming, I remember sitting in the film studio, waiting for a shot and going over my lines. The assistant director tapped me on the shoulder and said that my new stand-in had just come in. The stand-in I had been using had resigned, and it is considered etiquette for a star to approve of whoever will be doing that job. I looked over at this new man, my prospective stand-in, a job that leads nowhere and earns not much in either respect, money or possibility of advancement—a job that, rightly or wrongly, one associates with people who either have given up the idea of a real career or are using it as a stopgap to a life in a completely different area. Occasionally, a young actor thinks he can use it as a means to more important acting work, but he soon learns differently. I looked up and caught the eye of this new man. He smiled at me and gave me a gentle salute, and for a reason I did not understand, the moment hit me like a thunderbolt. I was not aware of his impending role in my life, nor that I had met him before, but I knew immediately this time that he was a very special person indeed. I had opened up sufficiently to see that much. I could tell instantly that he was a person outside my immediate experience. Perhaps I saw that there was no fear whatsoever in his face. Perhaps I could read in his smile and in his salute his lack of guile, his defenselessness. I think I could also sense an ability to love completely, a quality that I thought was not part of the human experience. I saw all this and for some reason felt instantly threatened.

I nodded to him and went back to my reading, instantly putting the moment and its questions out of my mind. We all try to ignore disturbances and wipe them from our minds, and this strong, open and gentle person was obviously a disturbance. I knew instinctively that he could take my mind off my work or my suffering, and I was committed to both, so I was obligated to forget about him. I do not remember the steps that led to our friendship—for that's the way we began our relationship, as friends—but I do know that I was quickly aware of his being virtually the only person I have ever met who felt just at I did about music, theater, films and literature—my obsessions. He had read what I'd read, listened to the same music I listened to, and was moved by the same things, and for the same reasons. And yet the passion seemed gone for him. Beethoven, Bartók, Thomas Mann, were life preservers for me. For him they seemed to be beautiful artifacts. Signposts. He saw in them only the reflection of the sun's light. For me they were not just symbols and reflections, but the universe itself. John did not minimize the beauty or significance of any work of art, but for him they were not the essence, not the source. *From* the source, yes, but not the source. Still, I knew he understood them at least as deeply as I did. This was disturbing to me. It was the origin of the first chafing I experienced under his teaching, for I was even then his student although I did not know it.

Why was this brilliant man not further along in his career? I would ask myself. What character weakness kept him from riches and success? I began to search him out for his flaws and could find none, outside of a kindness and attentiveness to everyone around that seemed to be time-wasting. I started to see similarities between him and my father—the brilliance and lack of worldly success. But my father has little self-confidence and great naïveté. John was devoid of naïveté and had a self-confidence so great that it didn't need any demonstrating. My confusion grew, but my regard for him grew also. We spoke of photography, and as with other art forms, we shared the same perceptions of what was good and why. He would sometimes borrow my camera and take a few shots with it. When the prints were developed, I found that his photographs were simple, loose and lovely. I asked myself why was he not a photographer, a profession with some dignity, an art form? Why did he have no ambition? Had he no pride? Sometimes I had the courage to confront him with one of these questions, and although I often didn't understand the answer, I could see that my queries didn't make him the least bit uncomfortable. In fact, he seemed to find them amusing. The essence of his answers indicated that he had no pride whatsoever, no need at all to express himself, and that his own unfolding was the only real statement he cared to make.

Around this time John informed me that he was a guru, a term that in those days was still not used very often, so I was neither greatly impressed nor appalled by this information. He went on to tell me of his few students and disciples, and began slowly to reveal some of the things he believed in. He spoke of auras, of astral travel, meditation, life on other worlds, reincarnation—and I became convinced that he was mad. Yet these were all things in which I secretly believed. Since early childhood I had felt certain that I could fly. For years, before going to sleep I would lie in bed and through an act of will try to force my body to rise in the air. Nothing came of it, but I never lost my belief in the possibility. In my teens I would sit in the subways of New York and try to project thoughts to other passengers. I'd concentrate on someone and try to have him look at his watch, scratch his nose or turn his head in my direction. It would often work, but I'd never know whether it had been through chance, and the effort of concentration was so great that I just stopped trying. But I longed to be a part of the next development of man, in which these supernatural powers would be revealed, and men would be one with each other because the contents of their minds would be shared—which would of course make conflict and war impossible. I had consumed enormous quantities of science fiction and prayed for the things I read about to come true someday. And now a man comes along, a perceptive, kind, gentle, loving, bright man, and tells me these things I dream of are possible, now, here, for me, for all mankind, and my reaction is to think that he is a madman.

Throughout all this the film is being shot, and John, without ever trying, gently and with great humility becomes its very center. Massaging one person's aches away, listening to someone else's problems, running an errand for a third person . . . always smiling, always at peace.

I begin to resent him. How dare he be at peace. I have the career, the money, I am the star of this film; why is he at its center? Why do people come to him instead of to me? He is, after all, only a stand-in. I begin to look for things about him to suspect. Surely he wants something out of this. I wait for him to ingratiate himself with the director, the other actors, the cameraman, the producer, but he is totally indiscriminate and will give to anyone, easily, quietly. His presence chafes and chafes. He strains all my beliefs; makes me question my identity. It is a relief when the film is finished and I can get away from the man whom I am beginning to love.

Shortly after *Popi*, I left for Mexico to play Yossarian in *Catch-22*. It was another role I cared very much about, from a book I loved, but the film took a direction I could not understand, and this became a source of great pain for me. We were in Mexico for four months, and we of the cast were left to our own resources for long periods of time, waiting for elaborate camera setups that literally took days to organize. Months went by with little or no contact with the outside world, and my lack of personal resources plus feeling at odds with the project in which I was engaged kept me isolated and on edge, so that I remained in an emotional limbo for most of the eight months it took to shoot the film. Although I suspect that a lot of things were beginning to formulate subconsciously, I don't recall spending one moment thinking about either yoga or John for an entire year.

I was in Los Angeles during the tail end of the shooting. I had an afternoon off and found myself aimlessly turning a television dial. I ended up watching the original version of *Lost Horizon,* which I had seen many years earlier, without much enthusiasm. The film is about a small group of people who survive a plane crash in the Himalayas and make their way to a hidden valley through an almost impenetrable mountain pass. The valley, called Shangri-la, is virtually a paradise on earth, and the body of the film deals with the varied reactions of the stranded party to this unexpected and perfect land. Some in the group immediately accept it, realizing it as the culmination of all their dreams; others, initially mistrustful, slowly learn to love it there and in the process begin to love themselves; while still others, yearning for the strife of the outside world, find it an evasion of reality and do everything in their power to escape. In spite of the film's seeming hopelessly childish and innocent, something in me yearned for the simplicity of which it spoke. This second viewing found me watching with my critical faculties shut off, for a change, and it lulled me into a degree of relaxation I had not experienced in months and months. The film ended and I turned off the set and sank back in my chair for several minutes, thankful for a reprieve from angst and despair, and for some unknown reason I decided to call John. I dialed his number, heard his voice, and found myself saying, "When I come back to New York I want to begin studying with you." I had not expected these words to come out of my mouth. But John seemed unsurprised both at hearing from me and at the decision I had come to. "What made you decide?" he asked.

"I'm not sure," I answered. "I was watching *Lost Horizon* on television and found myself calling you."

"What attracted you to *Lost Horizon?*" he asked.

"At the risk of sounding hopelessly naïve," I answered, "I think I feel the need of there being a place such as Shangri-la. I want to be part of whatever can help create such a place, such an idea, such an ideal. You and your yoga seem to be the only road to that end that I can see. God knows I can't find it anywhere else. I don't even get any peace from my work anymore."

"I am happy that you came to that decision," John answered, "and it will interest you to know that there is such a place as Shangri-la. James Hilton got the name slightly wrong, but it is there, in Tibet, and it is the center and home of the work we do in yoga."

The tie-up seemed too good to be true, too neat, too comfortable and safe, and after I said goodbye, the first of many doubts and fears began to well up in me. Analysis was finally attuning me to the hard, cold, brutal facts of human existence, and here I was responding to the time and energy of my good doctor by falling prey to folk law, superstition and madness! But I had found no peace in analysis, and although I had never experienced much of it, I believed in its existence. I believed in whatever it was that Gandhi had found, and Pablo Casals and Albert Einstein; they all seemed to have been living examples of what they believed in. They talked about peace, brotherhood, nonviolence, love, and their work and lives seemed proof that these goals were possible. What yoga seemed to represent was a manual whereby I could be reprogrammed. Where the wires in me, which were badly connected and poorly soldered, with frayed endings, could be retraced and reconstructed on clean printed circuits going round and round my system without shorting out, burning myself and others, mainly loved ones, in the process.

Past all the mystical talk and magic, this seemed the immediate practical possibility for me. I suppose my leap could take on the appearance of courage to some people. But I had no choice. There was nowhere else to go. For other people my action might look like cowardice. But to that I also reply, I had nowhere else to go. Somewhere in me I had a feeling of substance, of power and of meaning, and I had no way of finding it any longer, except from this man who seemed not only to possess these qualities, but was sure of his ability to transfer them to others.

Strangely, the days following my decision were filled not with elation but with defeat. I had asked for help—I had admitted inadequacy. It was like being on relief and at the mercy of the government. Like being an infant. An admission of dependency. A reversal of the American dream: the cowboy riding off into the sunset without even a woman beside him for comfort. But in the defeat, the humiliation, the not living up to a myth about American adulthood, came a stability that derived from my allowing myself to accept a fact of nature, a truth of existence. It is this: The idea of the self-made man, who "did it my way," alone in isolation, is all crap. There is no such thing. We are all tied to each other for life. And in asking for help, not self-help (which is mostly what analysis is: becoming your own image of what you want to be) but the help of someone who you admit is a better person than you are—in my saying to John, "I want to study with you," what I was really saying was: "I admit you are a little better human being than I am. I will follow your leadership gingerly and tentatively until you slip, until you make a mistake and prove yourself the charlatan you must be. But if by some miracle you do have a tiny piece of what you say you have, then perhaps you can spare a morsel for me."

Oddly enough, through the six years I have been studying, most of the important breakthroughs I have had have been accompanied by that original feeling of defeat. It is because we all, in looking for our power, our place in the sun, try to do it outside natural laws. Yoga places your system plunk down in the middle of natural law, and when your system is pinned to the mat, and you know the truth of something you have been shielding yourself from, in the hopes of special treatment from the universe, it is accompanied by a feeling of defeat. Afterward, you are allowed the power that comes from the acceptance of the truth.

I have to point out again, before going further, that I am neither sage, saint nor guru, but have come far enough along, I think, to talk lucidly about first developments. I'm a sophomore talking to prospective freshmen. These early stages are still clear enough to me so that I can most of the time leave out talk of God, the universe, cosmic energy and all the really heavyweight mystical dialogue. I am still grounded enough to be able to talk street yoga, or colloquial mysticism.

When I returned to New York I had my first session with John. I did not call him Guru for quite a while. I heard his disciples refer to him by the title, but I refused to do so, as I refused to do anything that smacked of regimen and formalism.

And John allowed this in me because he understood my need for elbow room. He knew I would not permit myself to be connected with anything that took away my freedom, even so far as wording and titles were concerned.

What I came to understand, over the years, was that what I meant by the word "freedom," and what the word means traditionally, are two completely different things. Normally, we don't think of the word "freedom" as an independent concept. We only use it in conjunction with the word "from." And then it must be followed by another word. Freedom from what? Mother? Father? White people? Jews? Earning a living? School? The word "freedom" is used a lot in anger, and what is usually meant is the annihilation of the object one wants to be free from. We think of the object as being the problem. Another idea of freedom is some kind of random, aimless, wandering existence without roots or purpose. In yoga there is further meaning. What John wanted me to be free from was *my conception of myself*—a task that is, to say the least, enormous. What analysis attempts to do is free us from our parents' conception of who we are, so that we can decide our own identity. In yoga this is only the beginning. Not enough, says the guru, to free ourselves from our parents and their conception of who we are. We must then get rid of *their* parents' conception of who we are, and theirs—and in fact, all civilization's concept of who we are. And when we have developed the courage to do all that, then we get rid of *our* conception of who we are. Then, says the yogi, we begin to know the meaning of the word "freedom." And finally we begin to find out who we are—who we really are.

None of this was presented to me on my first session with John. Nor in my first dozen sessions. What I was ready for were only some beginning techniques in meditation, which I was told gently to do once a day. These involved nothing more complicated than sitting quietly in a semidarkened room with my eyes closed for as long or short a period as I could comfortably handle. Initially, I was not even asked to concentrate on anything specific, but simply to allow myself to occur. I was to feel that whatever transpired within that space, internally or externally, was supposed to take place, and I was not to interfere. That was it. No mantras, no visualizations, no physical exercise. Just sitting silently and being. Freedom would have to wait until I was ready to tie myself to that which could make me free because it was itself free. But I did not know that then.

My first meditations, alone or with John, seemed meaningless. I did not meditate every day. I rarely meditated every other day. For the first six months or so, all I could handle was two or three meditations a week. I would do them at odd times, when there was virtually nothing else to do; when I was bored; or when I was depressed.

During the early stages little was revealed to me. The one sign I had that something was going on was that each time I sat down to meditate, my sinuses would drain. Certainly not a negative sign, since I had been bothered by swollen sinuses most of my life, but not to be equated with flying or visiting Mars, certainly. I continued my irregular pattern of meditation for months, adding an occasional mantra or two, given to me by Guru which, for reasons I could not fathom, did seem to relax me a little. But only a little. I did not enjoy sitting alone in semidarkness. I had the feeling that I would be leaped on by an armed murderer the moment I closed my eyes. I was positive that one of my children would start screaming for help. That the phone would ring with an important offer that would never be repeated. I was told by Guru to let my thoughts wander. If the phone rang, I was to include that in the meditation. If a dog barked, that, too, was part of the meditation. Dogs barked, phones rang, children called out for me, my sinuses drained, and for months I cursed the stupid position I was sitting in, thighs and back aching.

But then somewhere along the line I realized that I could

be *out* when I meditated. If a phone call was important enough, I would be called again. If my children were in real need, someone would look after them for the ten minutes or so that I was busy. So I started pretending that while I was meditating I was out. That, too, seemed to help. Then, in meditation one day, it dawned on me that I slept seven or eight hours a night without being attacked by a madman with a knife. If I had not been killed all these years under cover of darkness, surely madmen would leave me alone in the daytime. And surely I was more prepared to defend myself leaping up from meditation than I was in the dark, awaking groggily from a deep sleep.

These simple ideas finally penetrated my fear-thickened consciousness and after many months I began, just began, the process of meditation. I started to relax a little, my mind wandering into familiar areas—sex, career, money, family—and back again, over and over. But somehow, with my body in a relaxed state, the obsessional hold these concerns had on me loosened a little and I found myself discovering slightly new ways of thinking about things. During meditation I was able to solve simple life problems that were impossible to overcome on other occasions. Time started losing its stranglehold. I began to sense my own presence in silence as well as in activity. These things occurred slowly and over a long period of time, and I was not aware of a change taking place.

The first sign I had of something real happening was the realization that my most significant meditations—the ones that had me reeling with an airy, light-headed feeling, akin to that produced by really good marijuana, but without the physical weakness and lethargy that usually accompanies a marijuana high—took place when I was feeling good to begin with, at relative peace with myself. This seemed terribly important to me. It lifted meditation out of the area of panacea.

Throughout my work with John I had been troubled by the thought that yoga was a cop-out for the weak, that it was some kind of quasi-religious, goody-goody way of avoiding life in all its glory, its agony, frustration and triumph. But my new insight seemed to hint that yoga might be something more than that. If when I felt good meditation made me feel terrific, what would happen if I meditated when I felt terrific? Perhaps some of the magical powers I yearned for were lurking about in the really terrific states of consciousness. Well, this was exactly what I was supposed to come to. Guru, in his brilliance, knew, as he always knows, not only what to tell me but what I must find out for myself. And in finding this out for myself, I became Columbus.

One of the things Guru did tell me—and I subsequently heard his guru say the same thing—was that it was *not* necessary to *give anything up*. In the work, the meditations, the mantras, the time spent with Guru, when it is time for something to go, it leaves you. I dearly loved this aspect of the teaching, for it meant no moralistic wrenching away of obsessions and vices, harmful and not so harmful. No preaching and finger-pointing by the teacher. This simple statement of Guru's told me of the enormous confidence he had in his method, and also that he was not terrified by sin. I had long felt that many people in the religious life had placed themselves deeply in it because they were afraid of their tendencies in the other direction. Not so here. "You will give up the garbage when you see something more potent to replace it with," I was told.

I could perceive many of my obsessions as such, I could see that I was in their grip, that I was enslaved by them, but they represented the rare moments when I was happy and there was no way in the world that I would abandon the only friends I felt I had. There was no lecturing from Guru about my smoking, drinking, taking a great deal of marijuana; no talk of celibacy. It was just assumed that I would come to understand the power and joy his way of life could bring, and that by applying myself I could share this joy, and that the stranglehold these things had on me would be broken because they simply would not be as pleasurable as what I came to in yoga. Well, I would believe it when it happened, I told myself.

And then almost on the heels of my discovery that meditation should be done during optimum emotional times, I found that I had given up marijuana. I had not set out to give up marijuana. It was an old habit of fifteen years standing, and I enjoyed the relaxation it offered me; I enjoyed flouting the law, and having a secret cause. But to my surprise, one day I realized that I had given it up, that I had not had any at all for several months. What happened was that I was simply getting a better high from meditating, and marijuana had become a bore.

In these first formative months, several things become evident in my examination of Guru. They are all annoying. First, he never loses his equanimity. He is always unruffled and giving. I have never seen anyone maintain the same energy level continuously before. The same rate of speed, of interest, of concern. It does not vary or change for a second, and I begin to suspect it is an act he has mastered. I watch for a flicker of the eye to belie what he says he feels. I test him continuously, mercilessly. I wait patiently for meaningful Freudian slips, for avarice to rear its head, for homosexual tendencies, for some form of aberration. Some kind of crack in the wall. My analyst at least fell asleep during a session once, and I was able to hold that against him. Also, he took enormous sums of money from me, allowing me to believe that he did not care about me, that I was unlovable by anyone. But this man, this John, this guru, seemed to have no ulterior motives. I had to keep returning to the painful idea that he liked me, that he perhaps even loved me. Although that idea was too enormous for me to deal with consciously, the feeling started to seep through by osmosis. Not only did he seem to really care about me; he also knew who I was. Without flaunting his knowledge of me so that I would cower and be embarrassed, he made it clear that he knew more about me than anyone else in the world; parents, wife, analyst—somehow he could see me in a larger context than all of them put together. He knew awful things about me. Uncontrollable things that I hated in myself. He knew about them and loved me anyway. Not even in spite of them, but with them. It was continuously baffling.

There were books he gave me that I tried to read and was unable to understand. They contained ideas I could not begin to assimilate. It was as if they were in a foreign language. Guru would say, "You will understand this when your heart opens." I was revolted by this phrase. I felt that he was dragging me back to the Christian Science of my namby-pamby maiden great-aunt, whose religion was a way of avoiding all contact with life. Back to cheap valentines and faggy, pimply, Protestant Sunday school repression. I would understand when my heart opens indeed.

Yet he also gave me Hesse to read, *The Journey to the East, Steppenwolf* and *The Glass Bead Game,* works of art that fed me so deeply, made such profound sense to me, that I have touched no fiction in the five years since I read these works. They absolutely defined for me twenty-five years of looking and searching through the world's best literature; devouring authors whole, work by work, country by country. Then I read Hesse and it all stopped.

Guru showed me the work of Nicholas Roerich, a great painter and great mystic. His paintings hit me in a place I had never known before. And what I could not trust in life, in the direct glare, the countenance, of my teacher, I could trust through the filter of the canvases of Nicholas Roerich.

"I have mastered my craft," his work said. "I have mastered it and gone past it, without disillusionment." And then, further: "I have no need to paint anymore. I could live out my life peacefully without painting. I have no need to communicate to you with my paintings, nor do I even have the need to see the things that I am putting down on canvas. What I am seeing, what I am feeling, can no longer be put down with a brush on canvas. I continue to paint because it is a way of hinting to you a more important and subtler thing that there is to be found." His paintings were beautiful, masterful and inspiring, but mainly they were hints about something else. Not ends in themselves. He was painting from a vantage point that I was unfamiliar with. Mozart perhaps had some of that. I knew Roerich was in a place that was unlike that of any painter's work I had ever seen.

I tried to bring these people, Hesse and Roerich, back to my work with Guru, and they did spur me. I wanted to be that kind of artist. I wanted to communicate something perfect that lay behind ego and personal need. It is the finest thing an artist can do, and it is almost never accomplished. Somehow I always knew with the deepest part of me that it was possible to do this, but I saw little confirmation in the world around me. John knew this need in me and encouraged it. He also encouraged the states of exaltation I could find periodically in my own work, when I would momentarily transcend myself, become for an odd moment the character I was playing. This according to my analyst was a state known as "regression in service of the ego," a term I believe is Freud's own. When I first heard the term I was cowed by it and thought it was a diminishing of the highest points of my life, but being in awe of my analyst, I felt that my anger with the term was childish and was something I would outgrow.

I did not outgrow it, because as I now know, it is in these states that life takes on not only its greatest meaning, but *all* its meaning. And the knowledge that something can take us over and do better at our task than we can ourselves—that is what drives us. At such moments our egos do not regress; they disappear. And when they do, we and the task we are performing become synonymous. There is no questioning, no "who am I?" or "what am I doing?" We become the event, effortlessly and perfectly, and are capable of performing on a higher level than we ever dreamed of. These moments do not happen often, but when they do, we have the sure knowledge that they are perfect. And at these moments we are perfect within them.

With my limited resources I began to sense that there was something wrong with the phrase Freud and my analyst used: "regression in service of the ego." Those words did not give enough homage to what I knew were my greatest moments on earth. A preferable phrase, it seemed to me, would have been "annihilation of the ego in service of the spirit." But words like "spirit" were not yet in my vocabulary.

I decided to leave analysis, partly because I sensed that I was getting into places my doctor did not know about, care about or feel were part of the analytic process—one or another or all of these reasons. In addition, I felt I was outsmarting myself in several areas. I worked my way around my anger continuously, never got at its roots and was feeling more and more that I never would within the analytic process.

Also, I discovered that the best I could come up with philosophically was an uneasy existentialism. I found myself trying to say that life is devoid of meaning, that it is all a random joke, that we must laugh at the whole universe and once we have done so, go about our business and behave as if there was meaning. This was the culmination of twentieth-century philosophy, I wanted to fall in step with it, but I could get no sense out of it. It made me miserable. What I was approaching gingerly with Guru seemed, on the other hand, to be totally irrational, but it was beginning to make me happy, or at least peaceful for the first time in my life. I decided to opt for irrational joy rather than rational misery. My doctor and I parted warmly and amicably, and I thank him still for the work that we accomplished—the beginning tools for self-examination and an enjoyment of the process of change.

I continued to see John. Perhaps once a week I would travel up to Mount Vernon, where he lived in what he called his ashram, or spiritual school, with his lovely, unbelievably warm and happy wife, his mother and one disciple. I was for the most part uncomfortable in this environment. It was just too peaceful. Feeling capable of explosions that would be damaging to this place, I disliked it and was unhappy with myself. For there was no tension here that I could relate to; nothing askew, nothing hidden. In other words, I saw nothing of myself in this environment, and I kept looking for familiar things in the people and the place, but without much success. I came there because the tension I constantly felt was impossible to live with, but when I placed myself in an environment where it was missing, I was mistrustful and uncomfortable.

For a long while I was not subjected to being part of the group of students, friends and disciples who congregated there. If I met them, they would be more than cordial to me, but I misread their warmth as tacit proselytizing. I tried to lump these people together with the Jehovah's Witnesses crowd, but they did not match up. They were too solid. Their eyes actually saw something when they looked at you. I, for the most part, withered under their gaze. John, sensitive to my discomfort, would not subject me to this pressure, but would take me off privately and we would talk. Anticipating the things that were troubling me, he would lead me into ways of dealing with them that saved me much of the horror and embarrassment that I experienced in analysis in what seemed like full-time discussions about bodily functions and inappropriate emotional states. John knew the garbage and did not want to dig into it. He wanted me to reach for something higher and pull myself out of the mire. He referred to himself as a ladder that I was to climb.

It was a beautiful image, but I had no idea how to turn it into something practical. Often Guru's instruction would be similar to what I had heard when I was studying singing. In trying to make me understand how to produce a good head tone, my singing teacher had resorted to analogy, gesture and petulance. There was no lever he could push for me. I had to do it myself. I would twist my vocal cords into all manner of knots until by accident I did the right thing. Then my teacher's face would light up and my throat tension would ease. It took many dozens of attempts before I could keep the tone constant throughout my entire singing range. So it was in my work with Guru.

Using him as a ladder implied leaning on him until I found my own strength. I was not comfortable with the idea of placing my feet on his frame. Leaning on him, as far as I was concerned, meant revealing myself to him. Guru took this a giant step further by saying I must turn myself over to him body, mind and spirit, another idea that made me recoil in horror. Turn myself over body, mind and spirit indeed! The mind part did not trouble me too much. I had just spent seven years doing just that in analysis, and I did not feel I had much left to withhold from anyone. But body? That obviously meant homosexual weirdness, strange orgies in the shrine room. And spirit? That of course meant voodoo rites which would turn me into a sort of vegetable slave, visited late at night by my guru the vampire. Strange; I did not really believe in a spirit, yet I believed that he could perform "bizarritudes" upon it.

Guru tried to explain to me that much of my thought processes had become, to a certain extent, purified by my turning them over to my analyst; the same thing would take place on a more profound level as I turned over the rest of me to him. He would effect a process of purification on my system, and then return me to my true self, in a clear and beautiful form. I liked the sound of all that, but the trust one must have in someone in order to accomplish it was more than I had, more than I cared to have.

After I would calm down sufficiently, we would ascend the stairs to the shrine room, a darkened, enormously peaceful chamber filled with pictures of saints and sages from all religions, and many candles. We would meditate together and my main feeling afterward was relief at not having been raped either physically or spiritually. This was the extent of my trust for a long period of time. Slowly, month by month, I became less threatened by the environment. The shrine room became a haven rather than a chamber of impending horrors. I began to look forward to just being there, an island of peace in an insane world. Still I asked myself, when is the ax going to fall? When is money going to be demanded? When is he going to use me to get work? The answer came back in gifts from Guru, often things of rare beauty that he could not afford.

Toward the end of my first year, I had my first social evening at the ashram. I went alone since at the time no one in my family felt a connection with John or the work we were doing. Twenty-five to thirty people were there, and I dreaded going, as social engagements with a lot of new people were always painful to me. I was at the time a celebrity of sorts, and strangers at parties tended to treat me strangely. The more aggressive guests would give me long critiques of my work or tell me all about themselves, as if I were an old friend. The others would avoid me out of shyness or embarrassment. But the underlying feeling would always be a demand that since I was a successful film actor I had to be a certain way, and the end result was almost always painful.

On this particular evening I was treated as a human being, for the first time in years. There seemed to be an appreciation of my presence. All of them knew my professional work, and that I had been studying with John, but there was neither prying nor reticence nor embarrassment nor fawning. I was treated simply with warmth and respect, the way everyone on earth would like to be treated but rarely is. There was no sense of hierarchy; children were present, young adults, mature people and one or two who were quite elderly. All were equals. Even John got what seemed like no special homage. What I had fallen into, or been privileged to witness, was the ideal family at work. The air was filled with talk, laughter, silence, music, and with absolutely no feeling of cacophony or discord. As I read this back, it seems even to me like science fiction. How can such a place exist? How can there be on this planet people of this stature and simplicity? How can I ask anyone who reads this to believe in the possibility of this place, these people, when I did not believe it even in their presence?

God help us all, it is conditioning. We are, most of us, so used to treating ourselves and each other like animals, robots or slaves that we cannot see simple humanity when it presents itself. That's all I was witnessing. Humanity at work. Talking and listening.

It took months and months for me to begin trusting these people, but as I started to let down some of my defenses, I found that my vision of the whole world began to change. Yoga was a word that I had hardly seen in print, hardly heard of; certainly no one in my circle spoke of it. Mysticism was not a word in my vocabulary; peace was a concept connected with picket signs and leaflets, political campaigns; and Maharishi Mahesh Yogi had not come into full prominence. Yet suddenly everyone I met was somehow interested in and connected with what I was doing. Everyone had had some sort of transcendental experience, or thought they had ESP, or had a visitation, heard a voice once, or had deep spiritual yearnings. Suddenly I found bookstores containing nothing but books on mystical and religious subjects.

I began to see that the world was changing with my vision of myself. People were not as hostile as they had been a few months earlier. It was, of course, me. I was more open, more receptive. The world was just as it had been. And I discovered this truth: that the world is too big, too full, to conceptualize or encapsulate into a form or system. We all see only what we want to see; we accept of the world what conveniently fits into our limited perceptions. For whatever philosophy you care to follow, you will find volumes of brilliant treatises by the geniuses of the earth that will substantiate what you want to believe in. Life is meaningless? Great scholars will corroborate this idea. We are all gods? The crowning jewel of the universe? Mental giants will confirm this for you. Whatever you care to encompass with your consciousness can be affirmed by any number of brilliant thinkers.

I had always believed deeply in the need for brotherhood. For peace. For kindness and mutual receptivity. Here it was. As Guru would say, I was simply ready to experience it.

Around the time of this first loosening of myself, something happened that doesn't seem to be explicable in psychological terms. It was my first encounter with a new order of experience.

One day about eight or nine months into my work with Guru, I sat down to meditate in my study, a place where I was able to find a little quiet in the middle of New York City. As the myriad thoughts, ideas and fantasies filled my mind I noticed that they had sped up; begun to travel at a higher rate of speed than they had the moment before. It was as if my thoughts had been on a phonograph record that was revolving at 33⅓ rpm, and at this specific moment the speed lever was moved to 36 rpm.

It was not a dramatic shift, but it was disconcerting enough to throw me out of my meditation. I collected myself, settled and tried again. The same thing occurred. This time I allowed it to continue, and for the remainder of my meditation this odd phenomenon held my attention. Not my thoughts, but this new ability of my brain. I say ability, but ability connotes some kind of control. I was not in charge of this event. I could merely sit back and watch it take place. The meditation over, I returned to my routine activities unchanged, and actually thought little of what had happened until the next time I meditated. I sat down, closed my eyes, and once again experienced a speeding up of my thought processes. This continued for several weeks, and I got more or less used to my brain operating at 36 rpm. Then one day the speed was accelerated, this time to about 40 rpm. I was not as anxious about it the second time it happened. I began to perceive it as something developmental, and I became excited in anticipation of where it might be leading.

During the next few weeks I noticed a continued speeding up of my thoughts, until one day about six weeks after the initial incident, I experienced in one meditation a continuous speed-up from about 50 to 78 rpm; as if someone were moving the speed lever on the phonograph to its fastest position in one motion. It went to 78 and continued upward to a point where I could neither follow nor keep track of what I was thinking. It was now like fast forward on a tape recorder. Faster and faster my mind raced until the sounds and pictures were a blur, and then still faster until the tape played itself out and spun off into silence. My brain had come to a halt and I was left for the first moment in my life without someone yelling at me inside my head, or controlling me, or giving orders, or explaining things. No one was there; or should I say no one extra was there? It was emptiness and silence, and yet miraculously I was in some subtle way still present; silent and questionless, but still present. It was vaguely similar to those transcendent moments on stage when I was taken over by the character. And as I became comfortable with this wonderful feeling, something new happened.

It was as if the whole top of my head was gently removed, cranium and brain, and I was plugged in directly to the Milky Way. The top of my head became a direct channel to a view of thousands of stars, and I was seeing them not with my eyes but with my entire consciousness, as if all my senses had merged, become one and extended through the entirety of my body. This vision of harmony lasted perhaps five minutes, and when it was over I fell in love with myself. Sitting quietly and alone in a darkened room, I had given myself solace, joy and peace. It was the greatest imaginable gift, and I had presented it to myself. And what this brought to me was the first glimmering of understanding of a root axiom of all mystic teachings—in fact, of all religious teachings.

It centers around the idea of attachment. We must loosen our attachment to the physical world, we are told. But no one tells us why. Well, it is simply because when we attach ourselves to objects in order to make ourselves happy, we do not develop the ability to make *ourselves* happy. We depend on *things* to make us happy. And this covers craft as well. I had used acting as a vehicle for a transcendental state. That state was real enough, but what happened to me, what happens to most people fortunate enough to find transcendence anywhere, is a curious reversal of the truth. I bowed down to the craft of acting because it brought me to this transcendent state. Acting became God, and I worshiped its ability to transform and to elevate me. But the mistake is this, and it is oddly enough a humble one: it is that acting is not a thing. It is only an idea of something. In order for the craft of acting to live, I had to invest it with myself. This is true of anything we do that makes us feel terrific. I had done what we all do: we make the mistake of paying homage to the thing *we* have invested with life. *I* made the craft of acting transcendent.

What the great religious teachers are trying to tell us is that we must find transcendence within ourselves, independent of exterior objects, ideas, people—or rather, people as objects. Once we have done that, once we have found the key to transcendence within ourselves, then this energy can be placed in craft without feeling the sense of homage to craft, devotion to craft, terror at the absence of craft; we can paint, take pictures, act, play tennis, practice medicine, make love, and our lives will not be dependent on these things, because they become things we do with our joy. Not the reason for it.

This is an incredibly difficult problem to solve, let alone accept, and I do not mean to imply that with this one ten-minute event I had mastered myself. Far from it. Six years have passed and I am still grappling with it in various forms. But not as desperately. The hold that objects, crafts, people, have on me is terribly strong, and the habits developed over a thirty-year period are hard to break. But as my meditations get more beautiful, *they,* rather than the objects around me become more and more the point of reference for my life. What this one meditation did was hint to me that the peak experiences of my life, the transcendental moments on stage—which came, if I was lucky, once every few weeks for a few minutes—these feelings were available all the time, every moment of my life. My commitment to yoga and to my guru began to grow.

A by-product of this one meditation was that I found myself thinking from a new area in my brain. Before this extraordinary meditation, for the entirety of my life, I was aware of thought, all conscious thought, taking place in the front of my brain—in an area between and slightly above my eyes and to a depth of perhaps an inch. All cogitation caused a certain amount of pressure there. I do not know if this corresponds to medical theory, but it does not matter. This is what I felt. After the meditation I speak of, all my thinking seemed to take place farther back in my head, in a larger area of my brain, and the place I had previously considered the home of all my conscious thought was now vacant. This still remains true, six years later. And whereas before I was pretty much the victim of what transpired in my thinking, forced to act upon most of what was dictated by the little tyrant, this new thinking area was much more a friend. I could watch its operations as if from a distance, and begin to pick and choose the impulses on which I wished to carry through. A much healthier state of affairs.

The preceding section represents an outline of what took place in the first year of my work with John. I was a sloppy, inconsistent student, and my main attribute was simply that I stayed with it. I did learn a certain loyalty and a bit of courage, however, and by the end of the first year I began to meditate with slightly more consistency.

The loosening of attachments that I spoke of earlier was not much in evidence, except for my having given up marijuana, but a germ of possibility in that direction had been planted.

The mystical moment I had experienced would have to suffice for quite some time. It was a gift, I suppose, its purpose to spur me on, but the next period was pretty barren of these gifts. A prime motive for my involvement in yoga, after all, was magical power. I wanted to fly, I wanted ESP, and the ethical behavior so crucial to Guru was feeling more and more just like painstaking and laborious work. I yearned for some excitement in my life. None seemed forthcoming, so I forced myself into a sullen acceptance of the main precepts because I thought that they would bring me closer to magic.

However, I had to admit that my meditations, for the most part, filled me with quietude and peace, and as a result I found myself needing more of that peace in the life that surrounded me.

But my oldest boys, Adam and Matthew, were in a condition of tremendous turbulence, which became difficult for me to appreciate and understand. My wife, Barbara, was terrified of Guru, and did not see the value of my work with him, nor did she perceive what was happening to me. As a result I began to feel slightly isolated within my own house.

On top of the difficulties at home, the acting parts I was offered were getting less interesting, coming along less frequently, my reviews were not as good, and I began to really worry about my career. I was making a living, but not at a level that I considered worthy of my abilities. I spent a lot of time thinking about my career, which I confused with working. I felt that if I stopped thinking about working, the work would not come. A primitive and stupid notion, and of course worthless.

Along with these external factors, something was beginning to happen inside me that was very frightening. The anger I had not been able to exorcise in seven years of analysis was beginning to present itself, for reasons directly related to my work in yoga. It happened this way. My meditations were beginning to be havens of peace for me, little islands where I found no confusions, frustrations or self-hatred. At the conclusion of each meditation, I would throw myself back into low gear to prepare for the onslaught of life around me—low gear being a state of semidepression and wariness, which I considered normal and consistent with the turbulent life I led in New York City.

But as the months went by, the peace that I felt in meditation started to bleed through into the first minutes back in the world, and I would find myself engaged in social activities without my usual defenses in play. The children would yell, someone would give me a bit of bad news, and instead of expecting this negativity, I would now feel as if my hard-won peace was being ripped from me by the outside world and I would fly into a rage. Screaming, cursing obscenities, I began terrifying people all around me. I had them by the throat, I threatened their lives, it was all I could do to keep myself from beating them to a pulp. Thank God I had that much self-control, but the thought would be in my mind almost daily. It was awful and uncontrolled and frightening and I spoke often to Guru about it, but he would smile and indicate that it was all wonderful. This would throw me into more confusion and fear, because my behavior seemed totally inconsistent with the ideas he was teaching. My glimmerings of peace and beauty were turning me into an animal. It was a baffling and paradoxical time and the climax was even worse. In Los Angeles working on a disaster of a film, I had occasion one weekend to enter into a tennis match with some members of my family. My father was watching at the sidelines.

Now, I have always felt enormously competitive feelings

emanating from my father. Whether or not he actually had these feelings is not important, but I frequently found myself in positions with him where I would have temperamental outbursts and storm away, leaving him baffled and laughing. This pattern of behavior, I am ashamed to say, lasted well into my adult life. And what I was starting to feel was that somehow I was allowing him always to win, to joke his way out of joint responsibility for our disagreements.

Now, with my new-found abilities, somewhere in the back of my mind I was having fantasies about displaying this rage to my father. I would picture him cowering in the face of my magnificence, and once this happened, once he really began to take me seriously, my anger and rage would be purged for all time, and I would feel peace.

On the tennis court this day I was badly outclassed, playing against relatives who had for years been admired for their athletic abilities. Having my father watch me play against them was for some reason humiliating for me; doubly humiliating because I felt no encouragement from him. There were three times during the match when he shouted things, all of which I took to be derogatory. On his third interjection, I felt myself consumed with a blind white rage, a rage so intense that it loosened me in all my joints. I walked slowly over to him, my racket a weapon in my hand, and when I got within inches of his face I told him that if he opened his mouth again I would kill him. Somewhere I meant it, and he knew I did.

What I had anticipated was that in the direct glare of confrontation he would recognize his acts as hostile, but all I could read on his face was puzzlement and disbelief. I could feel the edifice of my anger crumbling with each second, and there was nothing to say, nowhere to go. I felt like puking. My relatives were shuffling around the court, hoping that they had not heard right, and my father was as baffled and hurt as anyone I have ever seen. I had, with blood lust in my eye and voice, actually threatened to drive my racket through his skull. It was not a childish outburst, either. I had spoken with the even steadiness of a born killer. My father continued to look at me, with pain, sorrow and disbelief, and as we stared at each other it became clear to me that the things I had held against him all these years were totally unconscious on his part, and that this great act of mine, which up to that moment I had considered the epitome of courage, was fast coming into focus as the most humiliating moment of my life. Instead of winning my manhood, I felt as if I had lost any possibility of gaining it. I knew instantly also that my outburst was beyond any explaining to my father or my relatives, then or ever, and that this beautiful rage that for years I had nurtured and cherished and protected was in fact the worst enemy I had ever encountered.

I now also knew why Guru had been so pleased with my outbursts, so encouraging of them. For years he had witnessed the tight rein I held on my aggressions and knew that if I continued to deny their existence, the built-up pressure would ultimately back up on me and cause major physical ailments. He knew, too, that since what I was sitting on was pure energy, in continuing to hide it I was keeping a good portion of my own powers from being used creatively. In addition, in order not to use these energies, I had to create a force field to encircle them, hold them at bay, and the creation and maintenance of this force field took even more energy. Guru's approval of my aggressive outbursts came not from a desire on his part that I beat someone's head in, but from the faith that I would not do so and the understanding that in order for the volcano to become inactive, it first had to erupt.

I vowed then never to resort to rage again. It was terribly difficult to keep that vow, but at least with that one episode, my homage to the beast was over. Which led to my being able to anticipate situations that were potentially dangerous, and deal with them before they provoked my rage. It took time and much work, but it was well worth the effort.

Shortly after this experience, Guru explained to me that there are two kinds of anger, one cleansing and the other not. I asked him how one could tell the difference, and his answer was, "By how you feel toward yourself afterward." And in order for me to understand what he meant, I had to experience both kinds. It was a while before I experienced the kind that cleanses. Even now I am not sure while it is happening. But there is indeed a kind of anger that is like a thunderstorm; it shakes up the atmosphere and clarifies and focuses a scattered environment. It is clear, clean, sharp, causes harm to no one, and is not a cover-up for one's fears.

The scene with my father stuck in my throat like a fishbone. For a while I felt as if my reaction had been justified, but when my rage dissipated it became clear to me that my method of dealing with him had been, to say the least, barbaric. Whatever he had done or had not done, he didn't merit that kind of treatment. I finally managed to write him a letter of apology, which he answered, and for a year or two our relationship was cordial but distant. In the past two or three years, however, we have fought our way back to a more comfortable relationship then we ever had, due in great part to my father's strength of character and ability to grow.

Guru once said that we have two natures, the lion and the lamb, and that most people embarking on a spiritual path think that they must destroy the lion. "It's not true," he said. "We must simply place the lion in service to the lamb."

Lama Anagarika Govinda, a Tibetan monk of great perception, was once asked how he felt about all the Western youths making pilgrimages to the Orient for the purpose of finding enlightenment. "Enlightenment is nice," he answered, "but it would be better if first they found a little peace."

Well, I was experiencing little in the way of enlightenment, but I was finding some peace in meditation. And these moments were becoming the focal points of my life. They were the high points of my days, my weeks, my months. But the contrast between the peace I found in meditation and the rest of my life was still so dramatic that I could not bring myself to meditate daily, let alone twice a day, which most of the people at the ashram seemed to be able to do. It was a wrench going in, and it was a wrench coming out. What I was embarking on was the long, slow process of examining my turbulent life in the light of my meditations.

In meditation my system felt unified. I felt no discrepancy between my body and my mind. My needs, fantasies, hopes and potential were all intertwined effortlessly, and my life's work was now to drag myself up to the level of my meditations. There was no magic involved. It was a very practical matter, for the meditations were real experiences. Now the peace and control I had found with the people and events running around inside my head had to be maintained in the physical world with people and events rushing around outside my head.

I knew that a part of this task had been accomplished when my meditations were no longer special in any way. When they were no longer a haven apart from my daily activities; when there was nothing internal to look up to. This would invariably mean that my life had caught up with my meditations, and there would then be a long interval when nothing seemed to happen at all, when the meditations seemed meaningless and stale. Time would go by, and then I would push through into some new area of peacefulness, some new perception about my life, and the whole process would begin again, but on a somewhat higher level.

While this was taking place, my relationship to Guru was also changing. Cracks were appearing in my defensive walls, and in some ways I tried to imitate him, but I still chafed at the idea of his being superior to me. We live in a democracy, and the idea of someone being superior was anathema to me. And yet when Guru said, "If no one is superior to you, what are you going to grow toward?" it made complete sense. Still,

I was filled with competition. There was none on Guru's part, and this caused me to feel even more competitive. I was living out my relationship with my father all over again, constantly jockeying for position, for who knew more, who was more loved, more talented, more spiritual. Surrender was virtually impossible for me. Fortunately, I could talk about this problem to a certain extent; yet nothing seemed to conquer it.

During this period I went to California to do a film. Guru came along as my stand-in, a job that paid little, and took him away from home, family and students. I am sure that he did this because I needed a great deal of attention just then. At that time, God help me, I found it fitting. And yet as the shooting went on, and my respect for him continued to grow, a part of me began to wonder why the most intelligent, the kindest person I ever knew was acting virtually as my servant. He would travel long distances to buy me healthful lunches, instead of my eating the mediocre fare from the commissary, and he would wash the dishes afterward; with his meager salary he bought me a Buddha, a beautiful ancient piece that I felt, at the time, was too soft and gentle a statue for my temperament. I had hoped my first Buddha would be something more fierce. And yet, though I was a bit disappointed at the form, still I somewhere sensed the honor I had been accorded.

During this time Guru's wife, Norma, bought him a beautiful ring, a gift that she had wanted to give him for a long time. One lunchtime he took it off his finger while doing the dishes, and afterward the ring was gone. And though John and I searched and searched, we could not find it. During the time John was washing the dishes someone had been in the room with us, someone connected with the film, and John was sure that the ring had been taken by our visitor. I immediately wanted to attack the person, not so much for the act of stealing, but because of whom he had stolen from. John helped me control myself, and then in the weeks that followed I saw him act in the strangest manner. John overwhelmed the suspected thief with kindness that was totally devoid of any undercurrent of hostility or need. It took years for me to understand the power of his approach, but it made a tremendous impression on me. What Guru did by his actions was to create a subtle bond with the man so that if he had been capable of repentance and growth, he could have found some way of returning the ring. Another thing Guru did was to detach himself from the object. With his warmth and affection for the man, Guru was making the ring a gift to him. Somewhere deep within me I could see the power of his actions, but on the surface at the time I found it weak and confusing.

Yet with all my inadequacies, misgivings and doubts, I must have been doing something right, because one afternoon on the drive home from work Guru informed me casually that I had become a probationary disciple. My reaction was shock and delight. It was to be a long time before the nature of discipleship would begin to become clear to me, yet I knew that it was a sign of my being pointed in the right direction.

This business of discipleship is complicated, and I must admit that there are aspects of it that still baffle me. At the ashram, in our community, there are at present about a dozen disciples. One woman has been a disciple for about fifteen years, her husband just became one. Their daughter has been a disciple since she was ten, and one of their sons was a disciple when he was born. I don't completely understand this even now, although these days I can sometimes see the opening that takes place in a student over a period of time, and have guessed or intuited twice now that a student was within months of discipleship.

I am aware that discipleship differs from community to community. No two teachers function in exactly the same way, and each ashram has a very different character. But this is as it should be. There are a great many personality types in the world. People have natural proclivities that pull them in one direction or another. A very physical person would possibly need a setting where Hatha Yoga, a yoga based on bodily exercise, was a part of the program. Someone who required a lot of discipline might gravitate toward a guru who was by nature quite strict. Some people need constant contact with their guru, others can find themselves through a photograph of their teacher, without ever having physical contact.

Each guru has hammered out his own road, and each disciple must finally hammer out his. As long as the disciple perceives his teacher to be a light-bearer, a bridge between his ego and his real self, he is on a path to truth. It is considered advisable to look around, to examine different roads, to explore. But once a teacher is found with whom you feel a connection, a teacher who can get under your skin, who knows who you are, who troubles and inspires you, it is then of great importance to give up the window-shopping and hang on for dear life. Sometimes people feel that in loving one's guru it is necessary to dismiss and despise all other teachers, all other paths. I am happy to say that we are not encouraged in that direction. My guru's guru was once asked to define the time when one becomes a yogi, and he replied, "When one is living by the main principles of all the world's great religions. Only then can you call yourself a yogi."

While we were in California, Norma came to visit John, and one week when he was not working the two of them took a trip to San Francisco. The morning they left, I woke up with a start. I looked at the clock, it was 6 A.M. and I had just been with them. I do not mean that I dreamed I was with them; I mean I was with them. It was an actual three-dimensional experience of some thirty seconds duration.

There is a lovely spot off Sunset Boulevard near the beach, called the Lake Shrine, belonging to the Self Realization Fellowship. It is one of the few places I have found in Los Angeles that suggest some sort of permanence. Most everything out there seems always about to be moved somewhere. Not the Lake Shrine.

That morning, the three of us—Norma, John and myself—were simply walking through the shrine, admiring its peace and beauty. This experience took place in what I was accustomed to think of as sleep, and yet it was as vivid as anything I had ever known in a waking state. It was both beautiful and baffling. Even more so because Norma and John had told me nothing about the route they were taking, what time they were leaving, nor that they were stopping at the shrine. I filed the event in my mind until such time as I could talk to John, and when I did speak to him the following week he confirmed that they had indeed been there. It was a thrilling moment for me. John was calm and seemingly unimpressed with my knowledge. He took it as a matter of course. It was thrilling to me because it represented an event that I had longed for, the beginnings of some sort of psychic power.

But as the immediate excitement wore off, I became slightly uncomfortable. I had not been asked to join them on their trip, and yet there I was. It was unlike me to go somewhere uninvited, to commit an invasion of privacy. And the extension of that idea was that if I was capable of joining them uninvited, then the same possibilities no doubt existed for them. They could probably be with me, sharing my life without my consent, perhaps without my knowledge. But there were large areas of my life that I did not want to share with other people, on whatever plane of existence. A large part of me was a Steppenwolf, and I cherished, or thought I cherished, my aloneness, my isolation. Guru had many times over the years referred to the responsibility of power. I thought it was a nice catch phrase and paid minimal attention to it. But here was an interesting little taste of it. I had been given a glimpse of a new power, and I was not sure that I was ready for it. If it represented giving up my ability to close doors, I wasn't even sure that I wanted it. Then or ever. What took years of painful work for me to learn was that the doors I shut to keep out others are shut most tightly against myself.

Although Barbara had now been with Guru and Norma socially on several occasions, she had enormous resistance to their overtures of friendship. Their presence in my life was a threat, and try as I might, I could not make her see their beauty and warmth. I was also finding it difficult to make her see the growth that was taking place within me. I found myself proselytizing more and more, something that our particular teaching frowns upon, but I was frustrated at not being able to share with her things I could share with John, Norma and one or two of the other people who frequented the ashram. I felt trouble brewing in our marriage. I saw the possibility of its collapse, and though I desperately did not want this to happen, the only way out at this time seemed to be to shut myself down and go back into the gray half-life that I had inhabited previous to my work with John—the area that I felt Barbara inhabited. There was no real joy in her life, and all I wanted from her was that she share the joy I had found, which in all honesty was not too much, but it was infinitely greater than anything I had previously known. John seemed to understand what she was going through, but from what I could gather, Norma was somewhat hurt by Barbara's aloofness. Norma genuinely liked Barbara, demanded nothing from her, wished her no malice and wanted only to be her friend.

One morning, Barbara casually picked up a book of mine entitled *Gandhi the Man,* by Black, Harvey and Robertson.

She read it in one sitting, and knew immediately what I had been trying to tell her for four years. She called John that day and told him that she wanted to work with him. We were in San Francisco at the time, and as soon as we returned to New York she began. She has made extraordinarily rapid progress, and I suspect she will outdistance me before too long.

Around this time, which was shortly after I received my discipleship, I had an experience that was somewhat similar to the great tape speed-up of the previous year. One day in the middle of a pretty ordinary meditation, I found myself vibrating. Not shaking as if with fever or fear, but vibrating as if my body had turned into a heavy-duty generator. It was not frightening; in fact, I almost thought it funny; and when I spoke of it to Guru, he seemed to take it as a desirable step toward something he would not define. Guru has often been very close-mouthed about things that I am going through, unless the experience has been frightening. I tend to overintellectualize, and he does not want me to think my way around my development the way I sometimes did in analysis. There have been times when Guru has used double-talk with me— complete descriptions of my psychic state in gibberish, with me all ears, trying to grab pieces of what he is saying. It is a trick that took me years to catch on to, and now when I hear it coming I know that I am in the middle of something I must experience and not work out intellectually.

The vibrating continued for several minutes and then disappeared. It came back again in my next meditation and continued for several weeks, whereupon the same thing occurred that had taken place with the tape speed-up. One day, for no apparent reason, the pitch increased. As if the machinery had become more sophisticated. Whereas the first experience had made me feel as if I were in a jet plane immediately before takeoff, now I felt like a fine piece of stabilized electrical equipment. Again, this lasted for a few weeks, and then once more the pitch was increased. This happened a number of times until finally I felt no physical vibration whatsoever. Guru finally told me that I was still vibrating, but at a rate so high that I could no longer experience it.

Exactly what this was I'm not sure. But over the years there has been a sense of increased energy in my system, gathered in meditation. The energy has become transformed continuously. It has gone from vibration to heat to a new kind of energy that feels like a highly refined electrical force. I will speak more of this later. But these first rumblings were, I suppose, the beginnings of my being able to gather myself as a sort of small power plant. If I recall correctly, this happened right around the time of my initiation as a disciple. (Unfortunately, I did not keep exact records, so my chronology throughout may be slightly out of kilter.) At the time I was not aware of the extent of the journey I would be taking, and there was no sense of a great pattern beginning to take shape. I looked upon all these events as isolated oddities, and although I enjoyed them, and found them exciting, I had no idea of where they were leading. However, a more detailed account would have no more meaning to anyone. People believe what they want to believe.

With discipleship, a whole new set of experiences slowly presented themselves, and with Barbara in the work, there began to be some unity in the household. We had a direction for the first time, and the peace that I had previously felt only in meditation or at the ashram now started to creep into our daily lives. But there were some new fears and problems.

For example, with Barbara's coming into the work and warming up to John, I began to fear that he would usurp my various roles with her; I was concerned that she would look up to him in ways that I felt she had never looked up to me, that she would have romantic inclinations toward him, that she would end up wanting to be part of his household and forsake me altogether. These fears all proved groundless, and I began to see how they were all things that had troubled Barbara

45

when I began working with Guru. Now at least we could share these fears, talk them through, and eventually learn to laugh at them.

There were times, I must admit, when I would see her blossom and flower as the result of working with him, and I would fill with jealousy. I wanted to be the one to awaken her to all things, and I would begin to feel that Guru's presence in our lives was a terrible intrusion. But then when I would see that this new growth and beauty in Barbara would be available first of all to me, and that rather than being excluded from her growth I was the first one to benefit from it, there was no way in which I could continue to harbor any resentment toward Guru. In essence, he was presenting me with the person who really was my wife, underneath the fear and the walls. Barbara had to face these same egoistic thoughts, of course, in my work with Guru, but we learned to share each other's joy once we got over the need to be the mechanism that triggered it. That, we finally agreed, was Guru's function, although he, too, refuses to take the credit.

Until now, except for one or two lapses into what could be dismissed as an overactive imagination, everything I have written makes sense in simple psychological terms. John could be interpreted as a loving father, or a perceptive psychologist. Meditation has now passed the tests set down by our standard-bearers of reality—the men with slide rules, tape measures and encephalographs. They have decreed that meditation does have some beneficial results, and so we are now allowed to believe in it; it relaxes us, lowers our pulse rate; it enables us to perform certain tasks better, and we seem to need a bit less sleep.

These are legitimate benefits, without a question, and in themselves they would be reason enough to meditate. But as far as the mystic is concerned, these measurable changes are only the beginning. For unlike medicine, yoga deals in optimum states—an area in which, according to my observation, medicine has little interest. Excellent health, joy, bliss, genius and love are not conditions that scientists tend to put under scrutiny. Medical men tend to work from agony upward to a gray region generally known as normality. But there are those of us who are capable of much more than that, in every aspect of life. And it seems to me that a proper area of scientific study would be the why of excellence. What goes into it? What are the personality types capable of joy? What are the series of steps that lead to ecstasy? An excellent life is no more an accident than falling down a flight of stairs or lung cancer. There are contributing factors to each and every aspect of our lives, and scientific studies should be made about all our optimum states. They are at least as important as the study of disease and mental illness. For without our knowing how high we can climb, even the norm starts to look like an impossible goal.

With discipleship, the bond between guru and student strengthens, and as it does, the excellence that is the guru becomes more and more accessible to the student. And the relationship starts to become so specific, so special, that there are no equivalents for it, no metaphors or similes, and in order to convey its importance and meaning, one must begin to use terms that are not found in books on psychology. These new words can be found only in religious doctrines. They are words that I am still not comfortable with, due to my agnostic past, and the ease with which they are thrown around by people who have no idea of their meaning. Words like "heart," "light," "spirit," "love," must come into play now, but what I have begun to discover is that instead of being vague, poetic similes,

47

magical placebos for weaklings, these words have at least as much reality as terms found in psychology, such as "transference," "sublimation," "ego gratification." Like their psychological counterparts, though, these religious ideas have meaning only when one perceives them at work within oneself. I hope I can convey at least a part of their meaning and a sense of how they begin to work on the life of a disciple.

Discipleship comes when the student begins to open himself to the power of the guru. The power that I just learned to generate in my vibrating meditations was there in enormous abundance in my guru, and on infinitely subtler frequencies. Discipleship meant that I had overcome enough of my emotional problems to be able to lower my shield and allow his energy to penetrate my systems, emotional, spiritual and physical. My emotional problems kept all sorts of things from getting through to me. They were literally a thick wrapping of insulation. And since the insulation was of my own making, much of my energy went into sustaining the shield. So not only was I not being fed from the outside; my inner supply of energy was held in check. As my emotional problems fell away, as my own psychic hands stopped pushing at the world, and most specifically at my guru, he and I began to unwrap the insulation, and it became possible for me to be fed directly by his power. In the simplest terms possible, this is what is meant when we say "the power of love." His energy was so strong that when I allowed myself to experience the full extent of it, I would often have to go to bed for an afternoon. I would on occasion think I was going mad, that I had internal third-degree burns, that I was disintegrating or being ripped apart, and yet in a day or two, once used to the new energy and openness, I would feel stronger, healthier and more perceptive than ever before in my life.

But with all the excitement, joy and wonder at what was taking place, with all the material for peace and growth at my disposal, I was still not keen on turning myself over to

Guru, "body, mind and spirit," a necessity if the work is to be done at its most profound levels. Although my trust in him was growing, it was not great enough, and the idea of such absolute surrender still conjured up images of eternal bondage. I was told repeatedly that turning myself over to him meant liberation, but it was a leap of faith for which I was not ready. And yet there was no question that with each area of myself that I did open to him, what was returned was more of myself. I was becoming more and more accessible, not only to myself but to all those around me. I found myself able to enjoy Barbara's success as an actress and a writer without being threatened. I could be strong and firm with the children without worrying if they would still love me; trait after trait that I had thought was an indelible part of my nature would be reshaped, tempered and adjusted, and often a problem would disappear without any conscious work on my part.

Yet my strong ego nature, that part of me which clung to isolation and secrecy, constantly demanded escape. I would often get sick of the teachings' emphasis on principled living, find myself yearning for freedom from what I imagined to be a boxed-in dependency on Guru for sustenance and growth. I still longed for an occult experience. One night I decided that I would leave my body once and for all, break loose from all responsibility. I wanted to escape. For a while.

I waited till Barbara was asleep, and sat down to meditate, not in the room that we had by now set aside for that purpose, but in a chair in the bedroom. I forced myself to breathe very deeply and rapidly, and repeated a particular mantra over and over, one which seemed to have profound meaning for me (for reasons that I did not understand, since it was a sentence in Sanskrit, which I'd never had translated). I kept up the breathing and intoning for what felt like ten minutes, and then I began to feel a pressure in my head at a point just between and slightly above my eyes. Instead of relaxing and making it go away, which was my instinctive reaction, I worked at intensifying the pressure, as if somewhere I knew what would happen. I kept repeating the mantra and breathing rapidly, and the pressure continued to mount and work its way deeper into my head. It began to feel like a thumb trying to break through skin and bone. It became more and more painful, and much of me wanted to stop, but I continued through the pain. The pressure grew, the thumb pushed deeper and deeper, and then in an instant I felt my whole head turn inside out, as if sucked through a hole created by the pressure. The back of my head came right through the front of my skull and I was left sitting in front of myself. It took a moment to adjust, but it was not nearly as strange as one would suspect. The room had been completely dark when I began meditating, not a sliver of light anywhere, but now I could see everything in the room with perfect clarity.

I stayed there motionless for a few moments, experiencing the room and my bodiless state, and then, out of simply desiring to do so, I flowed back into my physical self, which upon reentering felt more relaxed than at any time in my memory. It was a very pleasant experience. That's all. It was not wildly exhilarating, nor did it make me feel like Superman, and I never tried it again. This is strange to me, because flying, escape and magic were prime reasons for my getting into yoga in the first place, and now when presented with the possibility, I had not allowed myself to take advantage of it. It has been three years since that experience, and I have not allowed it to happen again, mainly, I think, because of the terror at having my meat left unattended. Although this event clearly indicated that I am more than just meat, that something else is at play, my meat still has a great deal of meaning to me, if only because of its familiarity. It's not even such great meat anymore, let's face it—a bit flabby, flatfooted, graying, balding, damaged by tobacco and alcohol—yet I must admit I am attached to it.

As I think back on that brief moment of weightlessness, which is still extremely vivid to me, it occurs to me that I was not seeing with my eyes; nor, for that matter, hearing with my ears. It was as if there was a unity to this subtle system, past any that exists in the physical plane. I seemed to think and feel from throughout my entire being all at once. It was a very good feeling. Simpler and more profound than the complex series of cross networks and filters that exist in the physical plane. It was too fleeting an experience for me to trust this feeling completely, but the memory persists, and remains very beautiful. Perhaps someday I will have the courage to allow it to happen again.

When I told Guru about this experience, he laughed and suggested that it could happen again. But I had lost the desire. It had occurred at a time when I was beginning to enjoy myself as a unified whole and I did not yearn to split myself up again, even in such a unique new way. Paradoxically, it probably came about because of my being more united with myself, and as this sense of integration continues to grow, I do not want to tamper with it. According to the teachings, this is the attitude one is supposed to have. Out-of-body experiences, ESP, clairvoyance, clairaudience, are all talents, to be sure, but we are taught to look upon them as side issues, signposts along the way. Getting caught up in these phenomena, using them for ends in themselves, is strongly frowned upon.

The great goal of the yogi is to be of service to his fellow man, an idea that was of very limited interest to me when I started on this path. I had enormous appetites, insatiable hungers that promised to have fulfillment just around the next bend. The moral basis of the teachings was of little consequence in face of the enormity of my cravings. The concepts, most of which can be found in a simple description of Hinduism, seemed far-fetched and strange. But one of the things that my excursion into "otherworldly" experiences showed me— in fact, what they were designed to show me—was that this extraordinary philosophy was not just an idea of life, thought up by some imaginative ascetics to put down rebellion among the peasants, but provable fact. Provable not on tape measures or x-ray plates, but in the laboratory of one's own organism, the only testing ground that has any real meaning.

The word "faith" came into play once I admitted that I had met someone who had gone farther than I had. John, I knew, had been somewhere that had made him a better, bigger person than I was. His being a guru was a vow on his part that he was capable, indeed bound, to take me along this path as far as I was able to go—if I had the muscle, as far as he had gone. In fact, there is no law that one cannot go farther than one's teacher. It has happened. But one must bear in mind that while one is growing, one's teacher is growing also.

The "otherworldly" experiences I had, some of which I have related, were exciting, and were also indications of my development, but more important, they all gave credence to specific points of this life philosophy I was learning. A few more of these experiences and it became virtually impossible to doubt the magnitude of what my guru was talking about. Little mystical dots of experience which when connected became a great arc of an immense circle. My hope is that in relating some of these experiences, I will communicate a hint of that circle. Had I the presence of mind in the beginning to write down all that occurred as it happened, with precise dates and times of day, it would not really have been of any more value. To the skeptic it would only indicate a more cunning imagination. The only real meaning this narrative can have is to instill enough faith—or if you prefer, trust—in the truth of what I am saying to induce a reader to attempt step number one, and see if that does indeed hold up one's weight.

If it is not yet clear, step one is simply sitting in silent communion with one's self and saying hello to the person within. Initially, it is not necessary to have a guru. What is necessary is the faith that through constancy and effort, enough energy will be raised by the seeker so that when the time is right the guru will appear. This is not magic, but a promise. We are all transmitters of energy, with the power to modulate, transform and finely tune the frequencies by an act of our own conscious will. It takes enormous patience without question. But it can be done. Finally, when we have tuned ourselves to a high enough pitch, we are picked up by a guru, whose work is, after all, to hear this call. Once our message is heard, we then can find our way to the teacher or he will find his way to us. It is a law and it is perfect, but we must feel worthy enough to put it into practice, and the practice is simply sitting down and doing it. I have no desire to proselytize. As I have said, we are not encouraged to do so. The work is difficult enough when one feels one *must* do it. If one thought he were being dragged into it, it would be all but impossible. I write this simply for those who feel that they cannot proceed without a teacher. I say proceed. When the teacher is needed he will be there.

The next three things that happened, over a period of several months, all represented tiny expansions of my consciousness. Because of my enormous rigidity, each was disturbing and indicates how much I fought and still fight my own development. As bad as my life was, as turbulent or depressing as it became, I was loath to give up the habits that created my misery, because they were my own. They helped me in my definition of myself, and no matter how flawed and imperfect that definition was, I did not want to tamper with my self-image.

The first event occurred one morning when I awoke and had no compulsion to action. My life had been for many years mostly a series of involuntary twitches over which I had absolutely no control. I had a decidedly animal nature, and was thrown into action almost invariably because of either some biological need or the feeling that something *had* to be done. I *must* buy a suit now! Make that phone call! Get a copy of this magazine! That book! That record! Not a moment can be lost! But in reality, very few of my actions had to be accomplished. If I took the time to question why I did things, most of my actions would have gone by the boards. But on the other hand, when I gave my actions great importance, they in turn gave me the sense of great importance. Going to the hardware store and buying a can of spackle took on feverish, earth-shaking dimensions, and being on stage assumed positively cosmic implications. Anyone who tried to thwart me would be ignored or yelled at.

On this particular morning, nothing had to be done. I lay in bed and my mind drifted over my possibilities for the day. Several things presented themselves and I reflected on them, recognizing that they could either be done or not. It did not make a hell of a lot of difference. After a couple of minutes, when nothing locked into place as an urgent demand, a *must do,* my reaction was one of terror. There was nothing to throw myself into, body and soul. What I was presented with was choice. Half a dozen things were equally balanced. And this ability to choose, calmly and in an orderly way, threw me into a panic.

In desperation, I called Guru on the phone, and by the time I got through to him I was practically weeping with confusion. I explained my situation and when I finished he laughed long and loud. When he stopped, he congratulated me and told me that I had just experienced the first free moment of my entire life. His laugh and the simple explanation calmed me, and I could then begin to perceive what had happened as a step forward, but in all honesty it was a while before I felt comfortable with this new ability. As I write, it seems probable that this event took place before my initiation, and around the time of the tape speed-up, but in the long run it does not matter. What does matter is that this freedom continued to a greater or lesser degree, depending on how rooted the possibilities were in earlier emotional problems. Even though my ability to handle them was now greater, old patterns have an enormous pull and it takes constant work to grow away from them. But I had made a beginning, and after a while the idea of choice became pleasurable, and gave my life more meaning. I was becoming the creator of my own existence rather than a victim of circumstance.

The next thing that happened was also related to the expanding of my consciousness. One night I noticed that I was no longer *dropping* off to sleep. All my life, sleep had been a deep, dark, silent place—a refuge where even dreams were not allowed to come and interfere. I paid a certain price for this oblivion, and that was back pain, headache and sinus trouble every morning of my life, because not dreaming—not recognizing that I had been dreaming—was another form of self-repression, and the energy had to go somewhere. I needed refuge in many places, and sleep was one of them. What it cost me in physical pain was worth it, I felt. Besides, by this time the pain helped to define me. I was Alan Arkin, that person who suffers on arising. It was an important part of my sense of myself.

But now all of a sudden my going to sleep meant simply turning a small corner. I was no longer dropping into a deep anonymous vacuous hole, and I began to feel that I had not slept at all. I would wake up quickly and easily, as if I had just lain down for a moment. There was no sense of having passed out, no pain upon arising, no adjusting to light, to the new day. It was terribly disquieting, and I kept waiting to fall apart in the middle of the afternoon or get sick from lack of sleep, but it did not happen. In fact, I started needing less sleep. There were no side effects whatever.

Again I called Guru, agitated and disturbed, and I said,

"Guru, a terrible thing has happened. I don't sleep anymore. I go to bed and close my eyes, but I don't lose consciousness." Guru did not laugh this time. "What do you want to lose consciousness for?" he asked, and the subject was closed. And with his one simple question I got a glimmering of what my life was to become. What Guru was hinting at was that in the future I could expect less and less refuge, until finally there would be absolutely no place to hide. Sleep would no longer protect me from myself; I would not be able to find oblivion in my wife's arms, nor in a darkened movie theater; not in food, not in literature or music. Wherever I went I would be present. This was a horrifying thought, because it meant responsibility for my behavior twenty-four hours a day, three hundred and sixty-five days a year, and I had a fantasy that sooner or later I would even be held accountable for my dreams, for my sleep. It was not too long before I was told that this was indeed true: Sooner or later I would be held accountable for what happened in my sleep.

No one wants to grow, I began to realize. No one really wants to know what life is all about. We want ammunition for cocktail parties, we want enough diversions to get us through the day and into the beginning of the next, but confrontation with self is anathema to most of humanity. Without the prods of my guru, I would be where he found me six years ago.

It occurs to me that what I am writing about is mostly the dramatic highlights of what has taken place over the past several years. I suppose I gravitate to these highly charged moments because of my theatrical background. From where I am now, these incidents have value mainly as narrative. They are to me now no more than bulges; knots in long strands of wool which are being used to make a piece of cloth. I am not a good enough writer, my sense of detail is not great enough, to give you an idea of the long strands that I am just starting to perceive, but perhaps they can be inferred from the accumulated events in this piece. I hope that I am eventually led to a sense of the whole cloth, but for now I consider myself fortunate in having come far enough to see some of the strands.

The next event took place sometime during the first year of my discipleship, about three years ago. And I cannot dwell on it without reexperiencing part of the fear it filled me with. It happened while we were still living in New York City. One afternoon my son Adam and I, along with one of Adam's friends, went to a neighborhood movie theater to see something that we were not deeply interested in, a time-filler. I do not remember the name of the film, but it was in French, and was somewhat violent. Toward the climax, when I was quite absorbed in the film, an event totally unrelated to what I was seeing on the screen blasted its way into my head. As if in a daydream, I pictured myself—or rather saw and felt it simultaneously—being dragged up a short set of wooden stairs onto a platform. The platform and stairs were makeshift and in the middle of a town square. It was night. A screaming mob held torches, and I was about to have something awful done to me. What was about to happen was on the tip of my mind, but I did not care to either picture it or verbalize it to myself. I knew that the place was France, and I knew also that it was an earlier era. The event lasted perhaps three or four seconds, but its effect on me was enormous. I was filled with great fear—the hair stood up on the back of my neck—and I was forced to leave the theater.

But in this emotional state I still had enough presence of mind to examine what had just taken place. If it was a fantasy, it was unlike any I had ever experienced. First of all, since I am connected with film, I tend to be highly concentrated when I am watching one. My mind does not wander. Secondly, my fantasies are all on the same energy level as the thoughts that surround them. I think this has always been the case. They come and go, abruptly perhaps, but still they fit comfortably into the energy stream of the thoughts in front of and behind the fantasy. And I do not tend to be shocked at my own fantasies. This event, however, came into my head like a thunderbolt. It was like an analytic breakthrough. It came crashing into my consciousness uninvited and left me gasping for breath. The obvious psychological tie-in, which I gravitated toward, was to think that it was inspired by the violent French film I had been watching. I questioned whether the movie triggered this response, but my fantasy was infinitely too vivid, too graphic, too harrowing. My fantasies invariably fed something in me. This fed nothing. It was an unwelcome intrusion.

I went home troubled by the experience. What I could not help feeling was that I had for a moment glimpsed something from an earlier life. A taste of reincarnation. This was a topic that Guru had brought up on several occasions, but somewhere in me I rebelled at the idea. It was too irrational. We are born and we die. Reincarnation seemed to me to be an easy way of avoiding the awesome fact of one's death—the total obliteration of consciousness, the eternal end, worms eating through flesh, all that. And yet I had, just a short time earlier, experienced a brief moment outside my own body, which certainly raised questions. What was this consciousness of mine, which could live even for a brief time outside the flesh? I was unequipped to answer this, and yet reluctant to accept the answers that rolled so easily out of Guru's mouth. But here I was, presented with something that seemed on the face of it to have no other explanation. With my new strength and somewhat greater ability to perceive myself and the world around me, I could not accept its being a step backward.

I decided to test Guru's powers. He had mentioned at one point that a guru must have some knowledge of at least three former lives of each student. If what I had experienced was related to a former incarnation, and if his knowledge of me was as great as he intimated, then he would know what had happened to me. Guru and I had never for a moment discussed my former lives, and I don't think the word "France" had ever passed my lips in his presence.

I drove to his house the next day. When we were alone I asked him this question, phrased exactly this way (I remember it vividly, because I wanted to couch my questions in such a way as to give out very little information). "Was I connected with the French Revolution?" He smiled the smile that I have come to know so well, a smile that at once is congratulatory and tells me that he knows ten times more about the subject than he can talk about. "Yes," he answered. "Something terrible happened, didn't it?" I asked. This was all I said. A vague, rather general question. He smiled again and then said just this: "Do you have trouble shaving in the morning?" Once again the hair rose on the back of my neck. The night before, I had been in the French Revolution, on the verge of being decapitated by a mob. I could sense the blood lust of my captors, and could now see a shadowy guillotine. The crowd and my captors were past any human feeling, and seemed to me like beasts in a jungle. I sensed also that I was not an evil person, and that although the event of my execution was not totally unexpected, I was nevertheless being done an injustice. Mercifully, in my memory I was spared the moment of my beheading. (That vision was saved for the following year.)

Yes, I did have trouble shaving in the morning. Knives, razors, hatchets . . . they were all difficult for me. I did not like sharp blades, and this discomfort I had become used to thinking of in analytic terms—unresolved Oedipal feelings, castration anxieties, et cetera, et cetera—and each time I shaved in the morning, each time I was confronted by a sharp blade, I cringed, and then condemned myself for having a coward's nature and for my childish inability to be a man and give up these infantile neurotic patterns.

But now, with this new event, I was given to understand that what I had been shown, difficult and frightening as it might have been, was a great gift to accept and assimilate. I was grappling successfully enough with my violent nature to be allowed a glimpse of what had caused it. I was being shown one of its roots. It was indeed like an analytic breakthrough, as I had perceived before, except that instead of cracking open the immediate past, through hard work I had broken through to an event that took place two centuries ago. Whether from Guru, from higher up the ladder, from myself, or from a combination of these sources, it was a gift, and once I could accept it as such, I possessed material to further control my passions.

To complete this story I have to go back in time to 1965. It was the second year of my analysis, and I had been making quiet, unassuming advances. I was learning to trust my doctor and getting some basic techniques in self-examination, but nothing terribly important had surfaced. At the same time, without my being aware of it, a lot of deeply suppressed material was starting to push at me.

I was starring very successfully in a play called *Enter Laughing,* and in the middle of the long run I came down with a case of laryngitis. By this time I was sophisticated enough about myself to suspect that the sickness was attributable to the surfacing of some material in my analysis that I did not want to talk about. Nevertheless, in order to keep the play going, something had to be done to restore my voice. A doctor was recommended, a "miracle doctor" who was known for his immediate cures of laryngitis among singers and actors. I went to him. It was about noon on a Saturday, just before the matinee, and I was ushered right in. The doctor gave me a cursory examination, followed by an injection that I can still feel. I do not know what it contained—I suspect it was some sort of amphetamine—but it was as if molten lava had been poured into my veins. I do not recall the next few hours very clearly, but I know I felt like a rabid dog.

I got through the play somehow, but I raged, I fumed, and I wanted to tear the theater apart. I remember cursing a great deal, spewing out all sorts of venom related to my fellow actors, the audience and the management. I imagined I could literally climb the walls, and I am not sure that I did not attempt it. After the show I went back to my dressing room, feeling as if I had burned out years of repressed rage and violence. In this weakened condition, the walls of my subconscious came down and an enormous amount of analytic material started pouring out of my mind. I grabbed a pencil and paper and wrote steadily from four o'clock until curtain time that evening. Revelation upon revelation came to me about my early childhood, and by the time I finished I felt purged, spent and cleaner than I had ever felt in my life. The next day, Sunday, I dragged my good doctor away from his family to read for him what I had put down, and afterward, in a Freudian slip of his own, he referred to me as Doctor Arkin. He quickly corrected himself, but I took it as a great compliment, and a sign that I had done some significant digging. For a week I felt clean and whole and pure.

The following Saturday I got to the theater a half hour before the show, took a few minutes to shake off the outside world and locate my character, and then got ready to shave. Now, at this theater, as in many theaters, there is a backstage sound system that allows the actors in their dressing rooms to hear the audience and the action on stage, and also to get time checks from the stage manager. It allows the actors to stay in their dressing rooms rather than wait in the wings. I picked up my razor, held it against my face, and at that precise moment the sound system was turned on. What I heard was the roar of the matinee audience scrambling for seats, but the juxtaposition of the two things—the razor against my face and the noise of the crowd—caused my hands and then my feet to go absolutely dead. I did not know what was wrong with me. I shook myself several times to get the circulation going, but it did not help. I felt as if I was in terrible jeopardy, and I could not bring myself either to shave or to go on stage.

For a half hour I sat paralyzed in my dressing room, and then, with much coaxing from the stage manager, I finally managed to get dressed and stagger through the performance, after a twenty-minute delay of the curtain. From that moment until the end of the run six months later, the idea of going on stage filled me with mortal dread. I tried pills and I tried alcohol, and the combination of the two in great quantities finally got me through each performance. But even worse than the fear was the idea that all the analytical material that I had uncovered, instead of helping and freeing me, had actually thrown me into a worse state than I was in before. Now I could not function in the work that I loved and needed.

I tried attacking the problem in my doctor's office with all my intelligence and courage, but it was no use. My doctor referred to what I was experiencing as homosexual panic: the fear of being a homosexual. I tried to accept that idea, to put it to work for me somehow, and I forced myself to think of fantasies and frightening memories that might shed light on the problem, but nothing helped. Throughout the rest of my analysis this problem persisted and I came to the unhappy conclusion that pain was the end result of truth. But I know now, in light of subsequent events, that what I had actually experienced was a crack in the wall so deep that analysis had no way of helping me. The fear I had experienced was an awful memory dredged up from a life some two hundred years ago and there was no way in the world that my doctor could deal with that information. Nor could I at the time. It took four years of work in yoga to bridge that gap and give me an insight into what had caused that panic.

In the three years since the episode in the movie theater I have had one or two other hints at earlier lives, fleeting impressions that will not be pinned down and yet cannot be dismissed. But one other such experience remains quite vivid. It took place not terribly long after the event in the movie theater, and interestingly was also tied to the violent nature that I was trying so hard to exorcise.

It was at the time when Barbara had just begun working with John. She and I were meditating together. We were sitting across a small room, facing each other. It was the early part of the meditation, we were letting ourselves sink into a comfortable state with our eyes open, and we were looking at each other easily and warmly. As we did so, I felt myself somehow changing. It was as if another person was being superimposed on me, another identity being implanted on my own. It was a personality completely foreign to my own nature, and yet there was something oddly familiar about him. I am not a very large person, but I felt myself growing into something enormous; very fat and very powerful at the same time. I sensed that this person was quite cynical in nature, and yet mixed with his cynicism was a kindliness and peace. An odd combination of things. I also felt that I was an Oriental. As I became aware of these things within me, I saw Barbara's eyes grow wide. "Do you see anything?" I asked. How I sensed that something was visible to her I do not know. She said she could, and proceeded to describe in detail the person that I was feeling.

Now, I am an actor and a good one, but two things indicated to me that this was not a performance she was watching. First of all, I was not moving a muscle. I was in meditation and was completely relaxed and still. Secondly, even as a good actor, with a broad range of characters, I can always feel that a character I play is a variation on personality ingredients that are familiar to me; I can by backtracking arrive at the combinations in my own emotional makeup that have created this character; but this immense Oriental was outside my emotional experience, and Barbara described him with great accuracy. I was, she said, somehow terribly fierce and yet gentle at the same time. She could see my size, the fact that I was an Oriental with a shaved head, and she even described the garment I was wearing. During the event we felt completely at peace. Neither of us was at all frightened by what was happening. But as in most events of this nature, after the fact, when we felt that our concepts of reality had been altered, we began to feel slightly uneasy.

This time when I questioned Guru, I was a little less inclined to test him, but I still needed some verification that I was not losing my senses. Barbara and I told him what we had experienced and he nodded and smiled again, and said easily that I had been a Samurai who had become a priest. As he said it, the experience of the night before began to make more sense. It all sounded terribly familiar. And I knew somehow that I had become a priest not out of great piety but simply because I was sick of killing. From what I gather, perceiving a superimposed form on another person indicates the sharing of an earlier life. I saw nothing clearly happen to Barbara, and yet I had a sense that she was at that previous time a silent and devoted servant, a role that she decidedly does not play now. I sometimes have a glimmering of another form when I meditate with Guru, but it is not definite. I tend to think that there is something wrong with my eyes when it starts to happen, and I shake myself out of it.

I have tried very hard through the course of this journal to differentiate between that which I have actually experienced, that which Guru speaks about, and the concepts that seem to underlie the experience. It becomes more and more difficult to do since the three areas are starting to converge. And yet even now if someone could explain all this to me in another way, I think that I would listen attentively. The only problem is that the people who dismiss these events are invariably less happy than I am, and happiness is a gauge that I value very highly these days.

There was a time shortly before my discipleship when I was greatly questioning the work, and I asked myself what my reaction would be if I found out that Guru was a complete fraud, that he had duped me for my money or was just plain insane. I thought long and hard about this and decided that if that were the case, then my reaction would be one of great pity. "How can this be?" I would ask myself. "The man is a cheat, a liar and a fraud. How can you not hate him?" "Because," I would answer, "he has made me so happy, and has not been able to do so for himself." Well, of course, with that I knew that I must follow him, because it meant that even in my worst fears, no matter how I faulted the workmanship, the bridge that he created held my weight; which is ridiculous, because if the bridge holds one's weight, then the workmanship is good enough.

The two experiences of past life—the French Revolution and the Samurai priest—had an enormous effect on me. Both these events had been confirmed, shared and even elaborated on by Guru and by Barbara as well. Also, the experience I had as the Samurai, short as it was, was beginning to fill me with a sense of that former identity. I was acquiring elements of his courage and solidity and patience, new states for me in this life, and I was now forced to start thinking about reincarnation in a new light.

All my life I had felt that it was a crutch, another panacea for people afraid to face death. Now I began to realize that the opposite was true: To truly accept the idea of reincarnation meant to completely accept the demise, obliteration and total extermination of Alan Arkin. This thing that was my core, my through line, my essence, was something other than the personality, ego, hair, teeth, sense of humor, wit, talent that I had always thought to be me. And in order to get closer to that essence, my core, I had to learn to start wiping out my personal self. Having had a couple of small encounters with a deeper part of me, which seemed to extend past the birth and death of Alan Arkin, I realized that a crucial part of the work was to look for more ways of confirming this line, thickening it and extending it through time to whatever its limits might happen to be. What this hinted at, of course, was the idea of a "soul"—a word that I hated along with the words "heart," "love" and all the other symbolism that I considered instrumental in destroying half the world. But what other word would do? Spirit? Just as bad. I thought about making up a new name, but it would get spread around and end up being just as loathsome and misused as the word "soul." So to my great dismay, I found myself occasionally using "soul."

In spite of my having had a four-year head start, Barbara became a disciple within months of me. Once she decided that she belonged in the work, her commitment was very swift and her flowering was quite beautiful to witness. For a period of about a year after our initiations, the changes for both of us were more dramatic than at any time since. We were also presented with a lot of phenomena, but these have subsided considerably, though I'm not sure why. Along with the flashes of past lives, which Barbara also experienced on occasion, we began to see auras, or halation, around devotional pieces. Buddhas, statues in churches and even people with a high level of spiritual advancement could be perceived to have a soft white pulsating ring around their entire bodies.

There was even one episode of my hearing a voice in my ear, which caused considerable excitement, and another of Barbara's seeing a presence at the foot of our bed. The voice spoke to me one afternoon in our downstairs hallway. It whispered my name and a few other words of greeting. It was not my imagination or a hallucination. It was as clear and vivid as if someone was standing right next to me, mouth pressed to my ear. The house at the time was completely empty, there was no place for someone to be hiding, and the street outside was quiet and still. The whisper was warm and friendly, its purpose serious. I knew without a shadow of a doubt that the reason it spoke to me was to accustom me to this means of communication. It was a trial run. The fact that it has not happened again for several years does not dissuade me from this conviction, and I wait patiently for the next message.

Barbara's vision occurred early one morning while we were both still asleep. She awoke suddenly, knowing that someone was in the room. She glanced up and saw a bright presence standing at the foot of the bed and looking back at her. The face was translucent and the features were not totally clear, but she had the feeling that had she willed them clearer, they would have become so. She also sensed a profound and loving connection with this being, but the unfamiliarity of the event caused her to feel a twinge of anxiety, and as this fear surfaced, the entity faded away.

As we pondered over these two experiences, I recalled the many times that I had heard someone say, "It wasn't my idea; it came from a voice whispering in my ear." There have been countless references to such voices, from statesmen, scientists, artists and religious figures in all countries and from all times. My assumption has always been that the voice was a metaphor for the imagination or the subconscious. In that sense I could have said the same thing about myself numerous times. But now I was sure that the statements, at least part of the time, referred to having literally heard instructions from a voice— a clear, separate and tangible intelligence whispering in someone's ear. There have been people throughout history who have said this very clearly and without mincing words, yet we continue to mince words for them. We reinterpret and rationalize, and if we do not do it, then reporters and biographers help us in this task. But in the quiet times, in our rare moments of serenity and peace, who of us can deny having experienced some unexplainable event? Something that gnaws at one and cannot be dismissed or written of in materialistic terms? I have spoken to I do not know how many people who, when sensing that they will not be laughed at or thought insane, admit to having heard a voice, or having seen someone who could not be there, or knowing unmistakably that a distant loved one had just died, or that someone had been trying to reach them, or knowing intimately a place that they have never seen or been to before. If the climate is conducive to this kind of discussion, almost anyone will be able to dredge up a story that has had them in a state of awe for years. And if you challenge their veracity or make fun of them for being superstitious children, most people will shut down and agree with you, only to have the event surface again at a later date. These phenomena are not forgotten and they remain troublesome until we fully acknowledge them and give them a place in reality, whether or not we can accept what they represent.

Fortunately, Barbara and I had Guru to speak to about these things, and he assured us that we had not been hallucinating, that these visitations had been further gifts. Our work after all is to sensitize ourselves to subtler and subtler forms of energy, and these two experiences were simply confirmations of the work that we had done.

Some short time after this I awoke to a sense of Joan of Arc, and what she really was. It became clear that this poor, sensitive, devoted child who has mystified intellectuals for centuries was nothing other than what she informed people she was. In fact, by all historical accounts, she was initially as confused and troubled by her voices and visions as Barbara and I were by ours, the only difference being that Joan's visions were many and she soon grew to love them with passionate trust. She had no room whatever for discussion or doubt. Barbara and I were not ready for this kind of trust, but we were ready to fall in love with Joan and Joan's faith, and so we began immediately to look for a play to do that would express our feelings about her. It was time, we felt, to portray Joan not as an intellectual, or a military genius, or a great hulking lesbian, or some half-crazed ascetic, but as an extraordinarily loving, sensitive and advanced child who wanted nothing more in the world than to be with her family and tend her sheep, but who had this talent for seeing and listening and trusting and could not back away from the truth of her abilities and the entities that she was able to contact.

I saw all these qualities latent in Barbara, and I knew that she could portray them, and I also felt that I could direct the production. The play that most closely mirrored this view was Maxwell Anderson's *Joan of Lorraine*, and it was doubly interesting because it was written as if it was the rehearsal of a play about Joan. We were given permission by Mrs. Anderson to improvise and update the rehearsal sections of the play and we performed it first as a workshop production at a church in New York City, to excellent response, but as a workshop we were allowed only six performances. For a year Barbara and I tried to do it in a professional setting, and finally we got permission to do it at the Hartman Theater in Connecticut. In the interim, our feeling for the material grew more fervent. Our passion spilled over to our three sons, Adam, Matthew and Tony, all of whom badly wanted to be connected with the play. Adam ended up playing Dunois, one of Joan's generals; Matt played one of her brothers, and we even wrote in a small part for Tony, who was then eight years old.

Casting the rest of the play was enormously difficult. I knew that it would not be possible to cast people on the basis of their beliefs, and yet I needed some sense from them of a connection with the material, and a desire to both do good work and perform generously with the other actors. We wanted not only to express our beliefs about the character Joan, but also to create a kind of community to support our fragile theme. Since this image of Joan was based on her being in a pure and egoless place, we needed an environment where that delicate state could be silently encouraged. We also knew that this situation would create an enormous amount of heat and energy and that many people in the audience would not be able to handle its intensity. A shield would be put up by some and some would write off what we were doing as simplistic and childish. We found that in rehearsing the play we could stand to work on it for no longer than four or five hours a day. The actors would drop like flies after that amount of time, and feel as if they had worked twice as long. They did not know what was causing it, and I was not about to tell them, but since we managed to get the work done within that time, it presented no problem.

It was Guru's idea that the whole cast meditate every day during rehearsal, and I was very afraid of this idea. I felt that there were people in the group who would resent it, and that it might pull us apart. I kept putting off the idea, thinking that we should begin the meditations with our run-throughs, but Guru felt that they should start sooner so that the meditations were connected not solely to the idea of performance, but rather to the entire experience of the play.

There was an actor in the company who was a student of Guru's, and I asked him to tell the group that there were those of us who meditate, that we would be doing it during lunch break each day, and that anyone was welcome to join us. I asked him to make the announcement for fear that if I did it, it would sound like an official announcement from the authorities.

The first few days, a half-dozen people showed up, and as time went on it became clear that a split was developing in the company. There had been a warm, open feeling in the group, but now it was breaking up into two sections: those who meditated and those who did not, and the people who did not meditate seemed to be made very nervous by those who did. I started to feel as if the entire experience was turning into a way for Guru to inflict yoga on disinterested people, and I began resenting him for it, but I struggled my way through the resentment to where I could ask his advice on how to resolve this bind. Guru said that it was time to invite everyone again; that what I read as disdain was really the actors' not wanting to intrude on something they did not understand.

I called a cast meeting and said that I wanted once again to extend an invitation for everyone to join us in meditation. It was not to be construed as coercion, I explained, and went on to tell them why I had not done the initial inviting. I told them that meditation was simply a silent sharing of what we had up to then been sharing in other ways. The actors loosened up visibly, and began asking questions about techniques, how to begin, and I could see that what Guru had said was true. Most of the people who had stayed away had done so out of ignorance, not disdain or resentment. The group became unified once again, and almost everyone began to join us in our daily meditations. Many of the technical people joined us as well, and it reached a point where everyone began to look forward to this activity. Because of the play, and our approach, and the care with which it was cast, and now the meditations, the experience with this group became unlike anything I have ever known in the theater. It started feeling somewhat like the community at the ashram, with love spreading like wildfire.

The play was received extremely well. Barbara's work was radiant, a perfectly executed realization of what we had set out to do. And the rest of the cast followed her with passionate zeal. On the third night something extraordinary happened. I sat in the back of the theater, watching from my usual place, and as the lights came up I could see the actors were not doing what I had directed. With each entrance, something unexpected was taking place. Gestures changed, placement on the stage, timing and energy level were all different. I am a strong director and have a very definite idea of how a play should go, and my initial reaction was that my work was being willfully subverted. But as the play went on, I could begin to see that what was happening was unconscious on the part of the actors, and had infected all sixteen of them uniformly. The play had taken on a life of its own, independent of anything I had desired, and also independent of the actors' desires. I sat for two and a half hours watching this event as if I had never seen it before. After the play I went backstage to talk to the actors. I wanted to tell them what I had witnessed, but as we came together I could see in their faces that they knew. It was impossible to say anything. No words came out of my mouth. No one else could speak. We remained together, standing motionless for minutes, all of us silently sharing this sense of awe and joy. It was an enormous act of will to finally break apart and go our separate ways, and it was an experience none of us will ever forget.

The run proceeded smoothly and the empathy and energy continued, though nothing like that one performance ever quite happened again.

On closing night we had a small party, and I was presented with a gift by the cast and crew. As I started to open the box and placed my hand on the object beneath the tissue paper, it gave me a distinct electric shock. I removed the paper and saw an exquisite Tibetan religious artifact. In selecting the gift the cast had been sensitive enough to ask Guru what I would like, and the idea was his.

Four months earlier I had been in London and seen a Tibetan piece almost exactly like the one I was presented with. It was in an antique store's window and I found myself longing for it. I would pass the shop once or twice a week and hope that it had not been bought, yet though I could afford it, something kept me from buying it. It turned out that such an object represents a specific level of growth and must be presented to a student by his guru. I had not known any of this in London, but was unable to buy it for myself. Now it was presented to me in this extraordinary manner—from my guru, through the whole cast and crew of the most beautiful work experience that I have yet known. It became a wedding of everything in the world that I cared about: my family, my work and my studying with Guru. I was moved beyond belief.

Once or twice a year, John's guru would visit at the ashram, and it was always an occasion of great rejoicing. A party would invariably be held in his honor and the atmosphere would be one of open worship. No one actually fell at his feet, but it was evident that few present would have had any qualms about doing so.

His name was Ralph Harris Houston; he was referred to simply as Ralph, and he would accept the worship with simple humor and joy. Over the years I began to see that he accepted everything in this manner. A turbulent plane trip, a walk through the woods, a slow and bumpy car ride, a beautiful gift, even lip cancer and cataracts in his eyes, were taken with the same gentle ease, as was the heart attack that finally caused his death. There was never the slightest ruffle in his demeanor that I could detect. He had total and joyous acceptance of everything both around him and within him. For years I tried to discover the perimeters of his personality, some hint of where he began and ended, but it remained impossible.

When I visited his extraordinary home for the first time, I tried to measure the man by his possessions. I had always felt that what one saw in a home pretty well defined the occupant and on a first visit I would examine the paintings, the books and furniture and try to pin the person in some cultural and intellectual milieu. It works at least a good part of the time, but with Ralph it was not possible. His home was at first glance an extraordinary international museum of paintings, sculpture and artifacts. Tables were loaded with precious statues and objects, and each wall was filled from top to bottom with artworks of every description and period. It was like walking into the Metropolitan Museum of Art, until, upon closer inspection, one would see paintings and sketches that seemed amateurish at best nestled in with the masterpieces, and often in positions of prominence. The library was enormous and infinitely eclectic. A Ming dynasty vase would have a two-dollar wooden monkey peering at me from its center. At first it was baffling, particularly since none of it was done for effect. But after a while, as Ralph started to become clear to me, I began to see what his home was all about. Some of the things in his house were simply functional; some seemingly priceless objects had been bought at rummage sales for next to nothing. There were art treasures given to him as gifts by prominent people; other things were the work of friends, students or disciples, and Ralph valued them all equally. He cared mainly that the things be imbued with love. What had been made with love, or given to him with love, became part of the décor. He cared not one whit about its monetary value or what an art critic would have said.

At dinner I would often try to get his attention with an anecdote or a story, and although I knew that he was listening, I never felt that I fully held his attention, that I had really captivated him. It was slightly frustrating to me, and it is only recently that I realized that he had received not only the message of my anecdote, but all my other signals as well; and there was enough of him left over to have his attention on everything else in the room and, I suspect, on a dozen other things at the same time.

Recently I had an experience with my youngest son, Tony, that helped me in my search for Ralph.

On my last birthday Tony bought me a belt buckle that was like nothing I would normally own or wear. I was initially repelled by it, and wrestled with myself as to what I should do. I wanted Tony to know that I was grateful for his thoughtfulness, but I realized that he was sensitive enough to perceive my dissatisfaction with the object itself. I could not make a fuss over it and then put it away in a drawer somewhere. Sooner or later he would pick up the fact that I had been dishonest with him. After thinking about it for a while, I decided to be truthful. Even though I knew that initially he might be a little hurt, I felt that in the long run it was the best thing to do. I took Tony aside and told him that I really appreciated his thoughtfulness, but that the belt buckle was not in my taste. Then I asked him if the two of us could go back to the store and together pick out something that was more to my liking. Tony was wonderful about it, although his lower lip started to quiver, and I realized that he had badly wanted me to like the buckle. The selection had not been a whim on his part.

I let the event ride for a couple of hours, feeling as if I had done the right thing, and then it hit me that I had been a complete fool. What possible difference did my taste make in the face of this loving gift from my son? What was so precious about my idea of correct clothing that it could not be altered in the wearing of something that was a constant reminder of his feeling for me? I went back to him and apologized and told him exactly what I had come to, and I could see great relief and joy spread across his face. It was a great lesson for me, and in looking back, I can see that everything in Ralph's house was a reflection of this idea.

One small event gave me an even greater sense of Ralph's scope and dimension. Late in his life he suffered from cataracts, and when they were removed, the doctor warned him that he had to be still for a period of several weeks and not do anything strenuous. A disciple came to visit him from New York, and at one point in the afternoon complained of a pain in his back. Ralph told him to lie down on the floor, and then began to give him a vigorous massage. Another disciple, one who lived with Ralph and was deeply concerned with his welfare, called out in alarm, "Ralph, the doctor told you not to do anything strenuous!" Without stopping what he was doing,

Ralph said simply, "David has a backache." The other disciple called out again, "You will seriously damage your eyes! The doctor said you need months of rest!" Ralph turned to the disciple and said, more forcefully this time, "David has a backache." The topic was closed. A disciple of his was in pain, and his own comfort or discomfort, even the possibility of his own blindness, simply did not enter the picture. This was my teacher's teacher.

In the way that Guru spoke about Ralph it was clear that his surrender to his teacher was total. I suspect that it would be impossible to be a guru if this was not the case. On the occasions when the two men were together I would watch them carefully to see how this perfect surrender manifested itself, but strangely, there was little outward sign of what transpired between them; little indication of the boundless love that Guru felt for his teacher; and to my surprise, this seemed perfect. Somehow I understood.

In one of those rare marriages that works well and has done so for years, the outward signs of devotion seem to have fallen away, and the unity is expressed in tiny signs and in an effortless fluidity. It is evident that great joy comes out of this subtle awareness of two people for each other. One has the impression of watching a single thing with two parts, like an old dance team. So it was with Guru and Ralph. No fawning, no desperate attempts to please, no great public show of affection; only absolute unity. When Ralph passed away I waited for some sign of grief from Guru, some evidence of loss or emptiness; some slowing down or readjusting. There was none. Only a continuous and mounting sense from him of Ralph's presence. Guru saw little of his teacher while he was alive. The demands on each of them kept them physically apart except for rare instances. Since Ralph's passing, there is the impression that they are now together continuously.

Swami Rudrananda writes that there are points in one's development where it is a kindness to give up certain of one's friends. He says that there are those who refuse to grow, and to hang on to their friendship does them a disservice. It's like being at a banquet and allowing starving souls to watch you eat. There was a time three years ago when I should have listened to this advice. I saw myself growing at a faster rate than some friends of long standing. This is a process that takes place naturally in all of life. It can happen to us as a result of any number of things: a new career, an important new person in our lives, a traumatic event, analysis. If our friends are open and trusting, they will perceive the change as developmental and ask to share it so they may grow with us. But sometimes the leap is so great that our friends are unable to share it. Then resentment builds up, feelings of threat and alienation, and ultimately the loss of the friend. Also, if the development is new and unstable, these people's presence may be too active a reminder of past states for us to be comfortable around them. We have to be on very firm ground before we can extend a helping hand, otherwise we will be dragged backward into an old place.

Now, in the case of yoga, we are committed not to a thing, an object, but simply to the process of growth. Since it is not a tangible thing, something for us to covet and hang on to, it is natural to want to share it. In essence it *is* sharing. I wanted desperately to share my new-found wealth with these friends. I saw them slipping away from me, and did not want this to happen, so I pleaded with Guru, and he allowed me to work with them on a primitive level. I became a student teacher. At the time, I did not realize what a complicated test I had been given. I was in no way ready for this work, but Guru trusted me enough to let me do it in the hope that I would come to this understanding myself. He also knew that as an actor I was an imitator, and that in order for me to grow toward him, I had to pretend for a while that I was him. My teaching lasted perhaps a year. I was deeply committed to it, and to my students. In fact, I was so committed to the growth of these students that I used them as a way of not doing my own work. My way with them was intellectual and emotional, the only strengths I had developed thus far. Also, in a very subtle way it was a method of not surrendering myself to Guru. It was a way of keeping something for myself that had all the appearances of giving. The students were *my* students. In discussing their problems and development with Guru, I was making myself his equal, his associate rather than his student. With all the best intentions in the world, I had made myself into another image of myself. It was ego at its most subtle and deceitful, and the essence of why Jesus disliked the Pharisees. With all its outward appearances of giving, at the core it was completely self-serving and prideful.

My guru was so incredibly wise and kind that he allowed this process to unfold without interference, trusting that my underlying goodness would ultimately force me to see what was taking place. Well, to my credit I did some good with these people. I made myself totally available to them with all my meager resources, and they in turn made some headway. So much so, in fact, that they began to use more of me than there was, and I became drained and sick. I hung on and hung on, obstinately refusing to let them down, but my own weaknesses overcame me and finally, on Guru's insistence, I told them that I was no longer able to teach. It was a terrible moment for me. I felt that I had let them down, hurt them in some profound way. But what Guru knew was that, imperfect and shallow as my teaching was, it was for each of these people, at this moment in their lives, as much as they were capable of handling. I had, to the best of my ability, filled them with some hope, and though unable to give them the enormous energy of the guru, I had at least conveyed the knowledge of this energy and demonstrated its increasing availability to my life. This was not nothing. It meant that if they could get over the immediate feeling of rejection, then they would continue their search elsewhere and find their true teacher.

Two of the four people have done this, and I suppose it's not a bad average. After my initial feelings of failure, I began to see the enormity of what I had been allowed, the trust given to me by my guru, and his gift to these four people. I see now that for one to really teach, the *need* to teach must be burned out and obliterated. It is one more label, and one more ego need.

Earlier I spoke of this adventure as being a test. Years ago Guru made it clear to me that I would be given a series of tests to see what I was made of. I would not be told what the tests would be, nor when they would come. This instruction weighed heavily on me for quite some time. Who would be giving the tests? How would I know when I had passed? As time went on I began to see that all life is that test. Don Juan speaks of this in one of the Castaneda books. He says that the ordinary man is overjoyed by one event and thrown into despair by another. He says that to the man of courage, each event is simply one more challenge; something to conquer. In the conquering of events one becomes the conqueror of one's self. The guru's power is constantly available. One uses it to the extent one opens one's self to it. One opens one's self to it to the extent that one has conquered one's self, and one conquers one's self by becoming the master of the events that take place around one. This does not mean controlling external events, but controlling oneself in the face of them. This sounds initially as if one is being stifled, but it means liberation. One's life is no longer governed by fluctuations in the stock market, by what entertainment is available, by whether it is raining or snowing out, by good reviews, bad reviews, but by the incredible entity within that one begins to find by trusting in someone who knows that it is there.

I got my first glimmering of this entity three years ago. It was two in the morning, and I woke with a start to find that my heart had exploded. I was gasping for breath, sure that I was suffering a massive heart attack. Enormous heat and pain emanated from my chest. For some reason I immediately called

Guru instead of a doctor. I woke him up and explained in panic what had happened, and instead of calling an ambulance, which is what I expected, he congratulated me. My heart had opened. Once again I suspected his sanity, but I followed his simple instructions, and before long the terrible pain had abated and my breath came more regularly. However, the burning sensation that I had initially felt in my chest continued, not for minutes, nor for days, but for months and months. It would subside and then grow, and after a while I not only got used to it, but began to see that it was some kind of signal for the activities taking place around me. It became a new sense organ. In Guru's presence the burning would become very pronounced. In reading some particularly beautiful piece of literature or poetry it would flare up. In an unfamiliar place, a bookstore or a restaurant, I would find that a burning in my heart signified some kind of spiritual activity taking place there. It proved infallible. I felt even more liberated from my head, and began to let this burning act as part of my brain. I followed it joyfully and blindly. And then, all of a sudden, some of the writings that Guru had recommended for years and that I had felt to be mindless or general or dull began to make sense to me. And I remembered what Guru had said: They would make sense to me when my heart opened up. Well, my heart had opened, and it did not feel like Valentine's Day. It had nothing to do with greeting cards or vapid Sunday sermons. It was a physical reality and it was power. It was as if I had been given an extension to my mind; in fact, to my whole nervous system. A new wing had been added.

Until that moment my life had been my frontal lobe, my stomach and my groin, and in a sense my whole existence was based on feeding those three mouths. Now, suddenly, there was something new to feed, and for a while it was like a toy. I experimented with it, as an instrument for receiving and as one for sending too. One night at dinner I tried to direct a burst of energy from my heart to Barbara, who was about ten feet from me and walking away. I focused myself, concentrating on this new part of me, and she whirled around as if I had called her name. This happened not once but again and again, and eventually it became possible for her to do the same thing. This ability still continues, years later—I suspect it is permanent by now—but the burning has gone. This burning, it turns out, is a cleaning-out process, and when the debris has been cleared, the burning stops. My burning lasted almost a year, and when it finally ended, I missed its presence.

After the heart center opened, I became aware of this burning in other parts of my anatomy. Head, stomach, throat, upper chest—the entire system ultimately had to be opened up and cleaned out. Where this process takes place I do not know. How it takes place I do not know. But I do know that whether or not it can be measured by scientific instruments, it is at least in part physiological, and occurs in anyone who studies yoga for a period of time. It will occur in a student whether or not he reads about it, and whether or not he has been told of its coming by the teacher. It is a demonstrable attainment, the fruit of spiritual work, and its value is immense. These areas of the body that burn are referred to as spiritual centers. When each of them opens, one is conscious of mind flowing into that area. One is no longer able to think of the mind as a separate, independent organism, but begins to feel mind flowing throughout the entire system. It is an extraordinary feeling. Each time there is an opening one feels one's center of gravity shifting; weight distribution actually changes, and the body has to get used to itself. Initially each opening feels strange and awkward, and the accompanying heat, the burning, can sometimes be painful and uncomfortable, but as the centers get cleaned out, one feels more liberated, more buoyant and connected than was ever believed possible.

Until the time of my heart's opening, meditation had been a place of deepening peace and rest. I experienced the silent dark quietude of my soul in there, and I had learned to love it. Now, with the heart and other centers opening, my meditations no longer gave me refuge. They were no longer womblike gentle places where I went to feel safe and comfortable. Now they were continuously loaded with a new kind of energy, and I began to feel as if my finger was in an activated light socket, that an electrical charge was running through my system. Another of my hiding places taken away from me. Once more I complained to Guru, and this time he told me that I had better get used to it, that I had better accustom myself to it and grow up. There were no more hiding places. I grudgingly accepted what he said, and what has slowly happened over the years is that instead of yearning for that which I used to call peace, I now see that old place as a limbo where nothing at all was happening. It was a sort of coma. What the word "peace" means to me now is an ever-increasing connection with the energies of the universe. I am fed and nourished by this energized peace, by the hum of open fields, by animals, by the sky, by the sea and by the roar of silence, which is no longer an escape from activity, but the very center of a cyclone of power and energy. This energy continues to grow within me, and my life's task has become to feed this force. The more I turn myself over to my guru, the more I present myself to him, the more I make myself available to this power, and the more it makes itself available to me.

I know the great distance I have come in the last few years; I can only guess at what Guru has come to. He does not speak of his own development. The centers are like plants. They root in the spine and the flowers float in front of our bodies. I am told that once the centers have opened completely, one has graduated from the earth and goes on to the next plane of existence. A plane past the physical, where the body is no longer needed. I am also told that something to work toward is contact with one's master. A master is one who has gone a step beyond the one of earthly liberation, and has decided to curtail his own development and stay to work with people who are striving to better themselves. The word "master" refers to what they have done to themselves, not to our enslavement by them. These masters make themselves known only to those who have done an enormous amount of cleaning out. This is a difficult idea to accept, but mainly because most of us do not feel worthy of such attention.

We have come far enough in the past decade or so to acknowledge the idea of superior intelligence in the universe as being feasible, but why would someone who is able to escape this vale of confusion want to return voluntarily? The answer I give myself is parabolic. Why does someone choose to work with the retarded? The aged and infirm? Why are there people in the world who donate their time to animal shelters, to the children of the ghetto? To bums on the Bowery, the terminally ill? And why do countless people spend their time with flowers, digging forever in the soil, pruning, getting themselves scratched and filthy? All for the joy of seeing something finally open and bloom and take its legitimate place in the sun.

We earthlings see patterns and order everywhere in the universe—in the stars, the motions of the planets, the activity in a beehive, the motions of the tide, the design of a snowflake, a leaf, in strata of rock, in the seasons, in the behavior of animals—and yet if we cannot discern the possibility for order in our own individual lives, we decide that the universe is devoid of order. This is the absolute pinnacle of egoism. It is not a question of ordering the universe, but of ordering our selves within an ordered universe. I have seen that this can be done. The changes that have taken place within me as a result of my grudging acceptance of Guru's words have been so profound that I have no choice but to continue following his instructions to the best of my ability, knowing that my life has been given unity, direction and continuity by his teachings, and that each leap of faith I have taken into his arms has increased my wing span, which seems to be his greatest source of joy.

Postscript

I have to end this now, simply because if I do not, it will run on forever. Time has passed since the first draft, and I have impulses to correct and augment, based on my development since it was first written two years ago, but that would entail a whole new version which might be obsolete by the time it was finished. It is frustrating that I cannot contain this thing, let it settle, and yet the part of me that is person and not artist is delighted. It obviously means an accelerated growth, and the promise from my guru is that it will continue forever.

The purpose of this work has been to let you know that I am not unique, and that you are not alone. I send to you the love of my guru, which is the sole source of everything that I have found.